## Praise for *The Business of Good*

"I dare you to read this wild ride of a book and resist giving up your day job to become a Global Citizen. Jason Haber brilliantly captures the zeitgeist of today's social entrepreneur and shows you how to become a dynamic change maker."

—GAIL SHEEHY, AUTHOR OF *PASSAGES* AND *DARING: MY PASSAGES*

"Jason Haber has captured the energy, enthusiasm, and inventiveness of Millennials who have figured out how to contribute to the social good while doing well for themselves. Haber shows us where the heart of innovation lies. He persuasively explains that making a difference is good for business. Haber offers a dose of optimism just when we need it."

—FRANK SESNO, DIRECTOR AND PROFESSOR OF MEDIA AND PUBLIC AFFAIRS AND INTERNATIONAL AFFAIRS AT THE GEORGE WASHINGTON UNIVERSITY, FORMER CNN ANCHOR, AND WASHINGTON BUREAU CHIEF

"A revelatory and vivid analysis on the rise of social entrepreneurship around the world. Jason Haber depicts the new generation of leaders and entrepreneurs that are forging a new 'paradigm' based on opportunities that bring together market forces and a drive to make the world a better place"

—AZADEH TAJDAR, SOCIAL ENTREPRENEUR SPECIALIZING IN EMERGING AND FRONTIER MARKET STARTUPS

"Based on careful research and his own deep personal experience, Jason Haber tells the intriguing story of the emergence of a new model of doing good in the world, one that combines the business savvy of a startup with the social consciousness of a classic charity. *The Business of Good* is a must-read for social entrepreneurs looking for ways to create meaningful social change in the 21st century."

—STEVEN LIVINGSTON, PROFESSOR OF MEDIA AND PUBLIC AFFAIRS AND INTERNATIONAL AFFAIRS AT THE GEORGE WASHINGTON UNIVERSITY

"*The Business of Good* breaks important new ground as the first book that closely examines the why behind the increasing trend of businesses aiming to turn a profit while simultaneously transforming our world for the better. The author takes the reader on a thought-provoking journey using engaging examples with historical context to identify and uncover the roots of this phenomenon, and offers compelling evidence for its continuation and impact. This is a fun and engaging must-read for anyone interested in the evolving corporate landscape."

—REBECCA SHIN, SOCIAL SECTOR MARKETING STRATEGY LEADER & GENERATIONAL EXPERT, WWW.GENERATIONEVOLUTION.COM

# the business of good

## SOCIAL ENTREPRENEURSHIP
## AND THE
## NEW BOTTOM LINE

JASON HABER

Entrepreneur
PRESS®

Entrepreneur Press, Publisher
Cover Design: Andrew Welyczko
Production and Composition: Eliot House Productions

This publication is designed to provide accurate and authoritative information
in regard to the subject matter covered. It is sold with the understanding that
the publisher is not engaged in rendering legal, accounting or other professional
services. If legal advice or other expert assistance is required, the services of a
competent professional person should be sought.

**Library of Congress Cataloging-in-Publication Data**
Names: Haber, Jason, author.
Title: The business of good: social entrepreneurship and the new bottom line /
    by Jason Haber.
Description: Irvine, California : Entrepreneur Press, [2016]
Identifiers: LCCN 2015051269| ISBN 978-1-59918-586-6 (paperback) |
    ISBN 1-59918-586-5 (paperback)
Subjects: LCSH: Social entrepreneurship. | Social responsibility of business. |
    BISAC: BUSINESS & ECONOMICS / Entrepreneurship.
Classification: LCC HD60 .H287 2016 | DDC 658.4/08—dc23
LC record available at http://lccn.loc.gov/2015051269

Printed in the United States of America

20  19  18  17  16                                    10 9 8 7 6 5 4 3 2 1

*For Makayla, and the world that will be hers.*
*For Cory, and the world she has given me.*

# contents

# and now for the good news

*It may be that when we no longer know what to do,*
*we have come to our real work*
*and when we no longer know which way to go,*
*we have begun our real journey.*
*The mind that is not baffled is not employed.*
*The impeded stream is the one that sings.*

—WENDELL BERRY

Т**he** most significant story of the 21st century has gone largely unreported. It is told but only in bits and pieces. It's a hard story to tell, but what a story it is. It's the story of us—of how we've all been impacted by a higher level of social consciousness. Try selling newspapers with that headline. But it's real and it's changing everything. It has driven a hardly noticed, but hard to miss zeitgeist shift within our culture. Zeitgeist defines the prevailing mood or spirit for a specific period of time. Some shifts are amorphous: We don't know where exactly they came from or how they came about. But that's not the case with this one. We know exactly how it came to be. In this book, I'll explain it and define it. It's called *The Great Convergence*, and it's the driving force behind social entrepreneurship.

## IRAN, A GOOD PLACE TO START

I'm sitting in a coffee shop on East 47th Street in New York City with Azadeh Tajdar, a social entrepreneur with an extensive track record initiating, leading, and scaling social ventures in frontier and emerging markets across the world. It's 10:30 a.m. on September 11, 2015. Fourteen years to the day—almost to the very moment—when the north tower of the World Trade Center collapsed. We are meeting to discuss social entrepreneurship, whose growth has a lot to do with the aftermath of 9/11. We talk about technology, culture, Millennials, and the surprising commonalities between the youth of Iran and of the United States.

Our conversation turns to Iran, a subject she knows better than most. A member of the Iranian diaspora, Tajdar maintains close relationships inside the country. She was recently there and paints a picture of a place not so dissimilar from our own.

"Iran has an Iranian version of Uber. It has its own Groupon. It has an Iranian version of Amazon," she tells me. At the University of Tehran there are hackathons, startup weekends, and incubators for entrepreneurs. But nothing is quite as exciting as social entrepreneurship in Iran. In Tehran—or Tehran Valley as some call it—social entrepreneurs are working on a host of issues, from clean water to health care.

Tajdar teamed up with Leila Piran, a policy fellow at the School of International and Public Policy at George Mason University, to explore social entrepreneurship in Iran. "This is not something you read about in the West, but it is happening and it is very important," she tells me. This was the first time academics sought to evaluate and understand the Iran's social entrepreneurial market. Did one even exist?

According to their findings, there are between 50,000 and 75,000 active social entrepreneurs in Iran. In the first quarter of 2015 they worked with local partners in Iran to distribute a survey in English and Persian. Field work, in-person interviews, and further studies were conducted in April. Eighty-three percent of them are engaged in an initiative, organization, or startup with a social, economic, or environmental objective. Sixty percent believe using technology will help them find more effective solutions to their challenges. And more than half of survey participants intended to make social entrepreneurship part of their job, either through a new venture or by incorporating it into their current work.

Iran's social entrepreneurs have their share of obstacles to overcome. Red tape and a lack of regulation supporting their work rank among their challenges. In addition, the U.S. Treasury Department's Office of Foreign Assets Control (OFAC) restrictions have eliminated foreign grant money, halted impact investment, and prevented the growth of exchange programs with Iran. The Iran nuclear deal will alleviate some restrictions, but it is not a panacea for the country's social entrepreneurial community. Many hope the deal is the start of better days ahead.

The fact that social entrepreneurship is thriving in Iran should remove any doubt that the concept has gone global. It isn't limited to Western developed nations and developing countries in Africa. It is everywhere.

"The world is getting smaller," Tajdar said. "That has created a higher level of social consciousness."

In this book I've created a new prism for understanding the *why* behind zeitgeist shift. We'll peer into its fundamentals, its founders, its funders, its foot soldiers, and its future. But first, let's look back for a moment to consider how much our culture has changed. There are always perils in making cultural conclusions. There will always be outliers. There will always be Kardashians.

## THE MEDIA'S ROLE IN ALL THIS

The media is very good at reporting bad news. Film director Barry Levinson, who has commented on this phenomenon over the years, once told a group of graduates during a commencement address: "Let's use D-Day as an example. That was considered a shining hour where people sacrificed their lives for the liberation of Europe for democracy. Now, say television was there on the beach on D-Day. What would we report? Equipment broke down, soldiers were confused, some died by friendly fire, some couldn't reach their objective. What was wrong? Where were the mistakes? We would want investigations; we would want inquiries; we would recall General Eisenhower. Maybe he should be court-martialed?" The media is good at reporting conflict.

The media is very bad at reporting good news. "If it bleeds, it leads," the adage remains. That's tragic. Because of this mindset, we've missed one of the biggest stories of the 21st century: the rise of a powerful zeitgeist shift called The Great Convergence. It started slowly, but gained steam in the years after 9/11. If the media won't cover it, how do you tell the story of this historic shift?

A zeitgeist shift lacks the visuals of an uprising. So what we need is an uprising—no, make that two uprisings—one before our cultural shift and one after. If we could find two such events that happened at just the right time, then we could prove the theory of The Great Convergence.

Let me show you what I mean. Let's turn our attention back to Iran to better illustrate the world before and after The Great Convergence.

## JULY 9, 1999

In the summer of 1999, students at Tehran University took to the streets in a peaceful protest. Such action in Iran was unheard of since the 1979 revolution. However, the students were stirred to anger. The day before, the government had shut down *Salam*, a reformist newspaper.

Today it's hard to imagine students rising up to preserve a newspaper. But in 1999, before social media, and in a country with little internet access, this paper was all the Iranian students had.

The Iranian government struck back with brute force following the protests, beating hundreds of students and killing one. This set off five days of rioting in Tehran, mostly by young people.

"It was wild and sudden," one eyewitness recalled. Beds and personal items were set aflame or thrown from windows. The students called on people around the world for help. Their pleas fell on deaf ears. The Dow Jones Industrial Average had recently crossed 11,000 for the first time in history, and the Iranian uprising did nothing to benefit anyone's portfolio. Nobody cared about citizens whose lives were so far removed from their own.

The one exception was the *Economist*, which featured the uprising on its July 17, 1999, cover. Under the headline "Iran's Next Revolution?" it featured a 21-year-old protester named Ahmad Batebi holding up a blood-soaked shirt. The photo did not go viral (this was not possible in 1999), but it did nearly cost Batebi his life.

## ORDER IS RESTORED AND THE WORLD CONTINUES TO TURN

A few days after the beginning of the "revolution," order was restored, the protest leaders were jailed, and new laws were enacted to ensure that similar protests would not occur again.

The international response to the Iranian student protests was mild. The usual voices of condemnation came from world leaders. Individual citizens read about it (if they read more than just the front page, since it appeared on page A3 of *The New York Times*) and did little else. Frankly, there was nothing else for them to do.

It was also a busy news cycle. The day after the protests began, U.S. soccer player Brandi Chastain scored the winning goal to deliver the FIFA Women's World Cup to the Americans and celebrated by ripping off her jersey (this *did* make the front page of *The New York Times*).

## JUNE 12, 2009

Ten years later, Iranian students took to the streets again, only this time they found the international response to be anything but muted. In 2009, the world was a very different place. People cared and took action using new tools.

On June 12, 2009, the American media was focused on the H1N1 flu. The strain had been declared a global pandemic. Americans awoke to newspaper headlines declaring the health hazards of this potentially lethal flu. A smaller story revolved around the presidential elections in Iran. Most Americans had not spent much time following the campaign, even though Mahmoud Ahmadinejad, the anti-Western incumbent, was trailing in independent polls behind a reform candidate, Mir-Hossein Mousavi.

In the days leading up to the election, Iran's ruling regime became nervous. The government pulled the plug on Facebook access. At the time, Mousavi's Facebook page had more than 5,000 followers, which, for 2009 Iran, was significant. The Mousavi campaign used Facebook to spread its message beyond Iran's borders, as it quickly realized the election outcome may evolve into a larger struggle. "We are using new technologies because they have the capacity to be multiplied by people themselves who can forward Bluetooth, emails, and text messages and invite more supporters on Facebook," Behzad Mortazavi, head of Mousavi's campaign committee, told the *Financial Times*.

### The Role of Twitter

Facebook was only a small part of what was to come. Twitter played an even bigger role.

> Whatever happens today, Iran can never go back. You can't put this genie back in the bottle. #iranelections June 12, 2009 11:23 P.M. GMT (@oxfordgirl)

Several hours after the polls closed, Iran's election authority declared Ahmadinejad the winner in a landslide. But the results made no sense. At some poll sites, more people voted than were registered to vote. The number of votes cast exceeded the number of eligible voters in about 50 cities, and 200 poll sites had a turnout of more than 95 percent. It soon became clear that the fix was in. An Interior Ministry employee later told *The New York Times* that "the government had been preparing its fraud for weeks, purging anyone of doubtful loyalty and importing pliable staff members from around the country."

> Mousavi has called emergency press conference to dispute IRNA claims of Ahmadinejad victory. 11 P.M.: Africa Street/ Taheri; No. 76, Suite #1 2:50 P.M. June 12 (@TehranBureau)

At this point, the media reported the story, but it seemed to have little traction. This revolt was about to go the way of the 1999 version. Only it didn't go that way. Word of an uprising spread on social media networks.

> Ahmadinejad & his supporters will celebrate their victory today at 5 P.M. local time in Valiasr square & we will try to ruin his party! 9:07 P.M. June 13 (@Change_for_Iran)

> ALL Internet & mobile networks are cut. We ask everyone in Tehran to go onto their rooftops and shout ALAHO AKBAR in protest #IranElection 2:44 P.M. June 13 (@mousavi1388)

When the youth turned out in the streets to protest, the Iranian response was similar to the one in 1999. The Basij (local militia fiercely loyal to the Ayatollah) turned out to beat the students into submission. The plug was pulled on SMS messaging so students would be unable to organize.

But this time the protestors had two new allies. First, they had new ways to disperse their message. Just as important, they had an audience. Consider that for a moment. Even the best technology tools could not have powered the protest, dubbed the Green Movement, alone. The protestors needed people on the outside to receive the message, and to care about it. Now, even to their surprise, they had it. According to communications expert Clay Shirky, "Even if it's just retweeting, you're aiding the goal that dissidents have always sought: The awareness that the outside world is paying attention is really valuable."

> Students & people fighting back a large group of police & Basij right now at university of physics! I'm going to join them. #iranelection 11:34 A.M. June 14 (@Change_for_Iran)

> 2 A.M. and people still on roof shouting death to Khamenei. a week ago that was unthinkable. people very fed up. want freedom. #Iranelection 4:37 P.M. June 14 (@persiankiwi)

In America, there was a visceral reaction to the events in Iran. Users weren't passively absorbing information; instead, they were becoming part of the story.

When CNN failed to provide detailed coverage of the protests, a hashtag called #CNNfail was started. Users in the Twitterverse slammed CNN with a barrage of negative comments. "Hours after Iranian police began clashing with tens of thousands of people in the street," ReadWrite wrote during that chaotic weekend, "the top story on CNN.com remains people's confusion about the switch from analog TV signals."

> See #iranelection for deets. Short story: election went bad. Iran went to hell. Media went to bed. Ergo #CNNfail (@ ayse_london)

On June 15, Twitter planned to shut down temporarily for a scheduled maintenance. Just how important had the service become to the situation? The U.S. State Department formally requested the maintenance be delayed to keep information flowing into and out of Iran. Individuals also pressed Twitter to stay online.

> @twitter Twitter is currently our ONLY way to communicate overnight news in Iran, PLEASE do not take it down. #Iranelection 6:06 P.M. June 15 (@mousavi1388)

After brief contemplation, the service acquiesced, and users took great satisfaction in helping preserve the communications lifeline for

Iranians. With the situation in Iran quickly descending into chaos, users inside the country made sure the information got out.

> I am not sure if students killed in tehran uni dorm. uncon-firmed that there was shooting heard were attacked in streets by mob on motorbikes with batons—firing guns into air—streetfires all over town—roads closed. #Iranelection 2:32 P.M. June 15 (@persiankiwi)

> Bassej are out in force in darkness. this is when they oper-ate best. Streets are dangerous now for young people. #Iranelection 11:29 A.M. June 15 (@persiankiwi)

## The Role of Facebook

Twitter wasn't the only social media service with an active user base assisting those in Iran. On Facebook, dozens of groups cropped up in support of the opposition. Dispatches from The Associated Press were given as much importance as reports on social media. Word spread from group to group, user to user.

My brother and I sprang into action as well. Using our vendor contacts, we quickly created and produced a 100 percent eco-friendly wristband embossed with the words "Where's My Vote?" The wristband was the same color green as the Iranian flag. To market the product, we created a "Where's My Vote?" Facebook group that soon swelled to 1,000 members.

We took orders from around the world, and after a few days had sold several hundred wristbands. I reached a deal with the PeaceJam Foundation to donate all profits from the venture.

Of the 1,000 members in our group, almost all were under 30 years old. Many had never been involved in protesting a disputed election. Yet they had this incredible, passionate desire to help the opposition movement—a movement many of them didn't even know existed just days before they joined this group. They were so empowered, I felt as if they believed they could will the change to happen themselves.

Shahrzad "Shar" Javid, a vibrant Millennial, connected with our group on Facebook. Prior to the 1979 revolution, Javid's family led a privileged life in Iran, but they lost everything and were forced to flee when Khomeini came to power. Her family watched the 1999 student uprising on TV. In 2009, Javid didn't just watch events unfold, she took action, organizing rallies in Louisville, Kentucky.

"It felt good to be a part of putting Louisville on the map in supporting those fighting for freedom, peace, and democracy," Javid told me during an interview. "I'm a firm believer that every little bit helps, and it was interesting and heartwarming to have such a common interest with strangers, bringing people closer together."

Javid experienced the culture shift that has occurred since the 1990s. "I really feel like after 9/11, people, especially younger people, began voicing their opinions more and rallies began to run more rampant," she said. "After 9/11, people of all ages saw the impact of what such a tragedy had on people of every race, religion, age, and creed, and it lit a fire in so many of us to speak out and rally. It's amazing how different people reacted to the situation in Iran in 1999 versus now."

For the other members of our Facebook group, the "Where's My Vote?" page proved extremely important. Users from inside Iran sent messages to our members.

> We were in the streets near the place of Friday pray and they shooted (sic) pepper and tear gas. but we didnt run away. we scream: GOD IS GREAT.

Our members responded to this, offering encouragement and promising to do whatever they could to help.

On June 17, the Iranian national soccer team was in a World Cup qualifying match. Several players defied the government and wore green wristbands in support of the opposition movement. Such defiance was unheard of in Iran, and it did not go unnoticed.

> Football team protest was a big gesture as it took the message to every village in every corner Iran #Iranelection #Iranelections #Iran #gr88 6:08 A.M. June 18 (@oxfordgirl)

Ten years ago, a U.S. soccer player tearing off her shirt in celebration was of greater interest to Americans than a student uprising in Iran. Now, the image of Iranian soccer players defying their government was the most shared photo of the day in America. That tells you something.

## WHERE ARE WE NOW?

Even with a changed culture using new technology tools, old habits remain hard to break. Attention spans are still impossibly short. During those days in June 2009, the Green Movement seemed to get bigger and bigger. And then, as fast as you could say "thriller," it all faded into the background. It took the death of the most famous entertainer on the planet to shift attention elsewhere. "Many say that it was so unfortunate because Michael Jackson died," Tajdar said to me. "Momentum was building, people were talking about this electoral fraud, people were paying attention, and then he died."

Notwithstanding the King of Pop's demise, pop culture had undergone a metamorphosis. Emerging from the cocoon was social entrepreneurship. Its wings spread wide; it touched everyone from financial powerhouses like Goldman Sachs to nascent startups and nonprofits. It birthed a new era of problem solving that relied on the Business of Good. Make no mistake about it, problem solving can be a business. But business alone can't solve all the problems we face.

That's why nonprofits are extraordinarily important. Social entrepreneurs have disrupted the for-profit and nonprofit sectors by creating new business models for both. "Social enterprises apply business principles and tools to achieve social change, testing the age-old conceptual divide between profit and charity," Katherine Milligan of the Schwab Foundation for Social Entrepreneurship wrote in a paper on how the nature of investing is changing.

Over the past 15 years social entrepreneurship has grown at an astonishing pace. It has done so because of this zeitgeist shift called

The Great Convergence. It is the fuel that has ignited its leap from the fringe to the mainstream. It's changing the lives of those in the developing world and in the developed world. It's changing how we give. It's changing how we invest. It's changing who we are.

Welcome to *The Business of Good.*

# the great convergence

*Let's talk about the real world for a moment. I guess
this is as good a time as any. I don't really know how
to put this, so I'll be blunt. We broke it. . . .
Somewhere between the gold rush or easy internet
profits and the arrogant sense of endless empire,
we heard kind of a pinging noise, and then,
the damn thing just died on us.*

— Jon Stewart, at a College of William and Mary
commencement address

It all began with such fanfare. The biggest millennium celebration in history was about to begin. And why not celebrate? In the entire course of human history perhaps no other moment was filled with such peace and prosperity. At the close of 1999, there was much to toast. It was the crowning moment of a golden era consumed with Making Money Now.

August 9, 1995. This may have been the day the music died for Jerry Garcia fans, but it also marked the beginning of the Making Money Now phenomenon. The dotcom era was ushered into being when the morning bell rang at the New York Stock Exchange.

On this steamy summer day a new kind of company was going public. In 1995, the internet was a lot like the Wild Wild West. There was little organization, regulation, or order. Then along came Netscape and its internet browser, Netscape Navigator.

At the time, the internet wasn't a big deal. Worldwide, only about 16 million people used it. But despite the internet's relative obscurity, Wall Street traders saw something in this nascent technology. Netscape initially priced its offering at $14 per share. Shortly before the IPO was released, however, surging demand persuaded the company to boost the opening price to $28 per share. During a frenetic day of trading, Netscape shares soared to $75 per share before closing at $56.

And that's how the dotcom bubble began. By 1999, many Americans had attained a staggering amount of wealth. Some $10 trillion of net worth was injected into the economy. That's enough money to buy every single person on the planet a Big Mac, soda, and fries for more than a year.

Even the federal government enjoyed the largesse that came from Making Money Now. On May 15, 1997, President Bill Clinton signed a bipartisan deal that led to a balanced budget (in 2015 the deficit would reach $463 billion). It was an exciting moment for the country. I was on hand that day, as an intern assigned to drive a car in the presidential motorcade. I got to meet with President Clinton and congratulate him on the achievement.

During the late '90s, if you weren't making it big, it was a badge of shame. In the summer of 1999, *Newsweek*'s cover declared, "The

Whine of '99: Everyone's Getting Rich but Me." You didn't hear hardscrabble tales of how difficult it was to make money; this was an era when making money was easy.

Where were the voices of sanity? As *Newsweek* put it, "The strange thing is that nobody's really countering the money hype. In previous boom times in the 1800s and earlier this century, there was always influential criticism of such behavior coming from pulpits, schools, and colleges. Now it seems as if the list of deadly sins has been shortened to six."

Making Money Now became a cottage industry. Suze Orman released a best-selling book titled *The Courage to Be Rich*. Jonathan Hoenig delivered a personal finance book for those in their 20s and 30s called *Greed Is Good*.

One psychologist at UC Berkeley keenly observed: "People used to apologetically make money. Now you apologetically don't make money."

"It's the first time in the postwar era that so many people seem to be getting so rich with so little relative effort on their part. At least on the surface, it appears that the old work ethic has turned upside down," lamented former labor secretary Robert Reich. But no one paid attention to the naysayers. There was just too much money to be made. There was agreement on Reich's central point: It really wasn't that hard to strike it rich.

## THE BALL DROPS

On New Year's Eve at the close of the millennium, the U.S. unemployment rate stood at 4.1 percent. The stock market ended trading on December 31, 1999, at an all-time high. Champagne producers couldn't keep up with demand as the millennium drew to a close. By almost every economic barometer, the country was wealthier than at any time in its history.

American strength was projected not only by our economy, but also by our dominance on the world stage. By the turn of the century, the Cold War was long gone; America had no geopolitical or economic rival. Instead we had reached, some speculated, the end of history, and our future would be shaped by events smaller in scale and consequence than the Herculean struggles to defeat Nazism and Communism that dominated the 20th century.

In the run-up to the millennium the Israelis and Palestinians signed not one, not two, but three agreements that brought the prospect of peace in the Middle East tantalizingly close.

The U.S. normalized relations with Vietnam and expanded trade with China. In July 1995, the once unthinkable commenced in Russia: the Russian Trading System. Yes, even Russia had a stock market. It, too, caught the Making Money Now bug. The world was indeed a different place.

Making Money Now became an unstoppable force. It seemed nothing would halt its ascent. But on the evening of December 31, 1999, a different kind of bug posed a mortal threat to the euphoric times. It wasn't totalitarianism. It wasn't terrorism. Instead, it was technology.

The Y2K computer bug stoked worries of a coming Armageddon. To save memory, early computer programmers used two digits to denote the year (84) instead of all four digits (1984). There was genuine fear that computer systems around the world would go haywire, calculating the date as 1900, not 2000, when the century turned.

The public and private sectors spent more than $300 billion worldwide to fix computer systems ahead of the rollover to "2000." In Chicago officials estimated that the city needed to collect bridge tolls from 36 million vehicles just to pay for Y2K costs. Large corporations spent hundreds of millions to inoculate themselves from danger.

The U.S. and Russia set up a joint task force to ensure computer systems didn't misread the new date as an indication of an attack. The task force met for drills and stayed in near constant contact at the end of 1999.

On December 31, the world waited nervously for confirmation that no missiles had been launched. Other news out of Russia was largely ignored amid the celebratory cacophony of the new millennium. Late that evening Russian President Boris Yeltsin announced he was resigning from office. The first peaceful transition of the Russian Federation would commence with a complete unknown assuming control. On the evening Vladimir Putin took power, the attention of the world was, with good reason, elsewhere.

As the final seconds counted down at the end of the 20th century, the dream of a peaceful and prosperous future seemed real and within reach. The only worry was with our technology.

Little did we know, we had it all backward.

The moment arrived in a cascade of events around the globe. The new millennium first came to the small island in Oceania called Kiribati. A simple event with traditional dancing and a torch-passing ceremony marked the occasion. For the rest of the world, it was a more pyrotechnic affair. Millions jammed Times Square, the streets of Paris, Sydney Harbour. In Las Vegas they celebrated the new millennium not once, but twice (at midnight eastern time and then at midnight local time). ABC News anchor Peter Jennings spent 23 hours and 10 minutes on the air to cover this historic event.

The night was also remembered for what did not happen. There was no nuclear missile launch, and no doomsday scenario unfolded. That isn't to say Y2K was a complete dud. In Delaware, 150 slot machines at a racetrack failed to work, while the website for the U.S. Naval Observatory announced the date as 1 January 19100. Civilization would not come to an end on this evening.

And that's where the good news just about ended. Soon after the celebration receded, so, too, did many of the reasons we had to celebrate.

## THE HANGOVER OF THE MILLENNIUM

The hope of the '90s was soon replaced with something else. The next decade was bookended by a recession at its opening and another, even larger one, near its close. And between the crashes the news wasn't all that good either.

On the morning of September 11, 2001, Wall Street was set to open its trading session with the Dow Jones at 9,605. Eight years later, on September 11, 2009, the Dow Jones closed trading that day at the exact same number, 9,605. While at first glance the numbers might suggest the years between were benign, as we all know they were anything but placid.

It was a decade of cascading catastrophes. 9/11 changed everything. Katrina flooded New Orleans. The Janjaweed turned Darfur into a killing field. Global warming transformed the North Pole into a seasonal shipping lane. Iraq turned into an insurgency. Afghanistan lived up to its reputation as a graveyard to foreign empires. Homeowners prayed for a short sale, hoping to avoid foreclosure.

On December 31, 2009, the stock market closed 1,000 points lower than it had a decade before. First billions, then trillions of net worth vanished. Unemployment hovered at nearly 10 percent.

From 2000 to 2009, there were 13 wars, 21 civil and guerrilla conflicts, five coup d'états, and terror attacks in New York City; Washington, DC; Shanksville, Pennsylvania; London; Glasgow; Istanbul; Madrid; Mumbai; and Bali. More than 1 million casualties arose from these conflicts, with civilians constituting the vast majority. And those were just the events caused by man.

Mother Nature showed us little quarter.

Climate change reared itself in ways that felt apocalyptic, if not biblical. More than 700,000 people would fall victim to a never-ending cascade of natural disasters ranging from hurricanes, tropical cyclones, and earthquakes to heat waves, polar vortices, and tsunamis.

To say things were bad would be an understatement. When the decade mercifully came to a close, no one knew what to call it. Was it the "aughts," the "double-00s," or the "ohs"? No one was really sure. Most just wanted to move on and forget it ever happened.

In the years that followed the first decade of the new millennium, world problems got bigger and bigger.

But at the same time, something magical was happening.

## WEB 2.0

At first it was called Web 2.0. The concept emerged in the post-mortem of the 2000 dotcom crash. In the internet's first incarnation, users were browsers of content. With Web 2.0, users became creators of that content. This profound shift led to the birth of social media and with it the modern internet we know today.

With breathtaking speed new sites attracted millions of users. Social media completely transformed our culture in ways we are only now beginning to fully understand.

By 2007, social networking had achieved a major milestone: It was the most popular online activity in the United States. Even pornography was no match for social media.

The speed of social media's growth is nothing short of astounding. It took radio 38 years to reach an audience of 50 million. TV accomplished this feat in 13 years. The internet did it in four years. In 2013 alone, Facebook added more than 200 million users. In 2015, more than 1 billion people were logged in—at the same time.

Recently I attended an alumni event for George Washington University, my alma mater. I asked a friend of mine if she was going to go. She had no interest. "I have a reunion every day on Facebook, and that's with the people I want to stay in touch with," she responded. I suggested maybe some of them would be at this event, but I was quickly shot down. "No," I was told. "If that was the case, they would have posted it on their status updates."

Social media has enabled a level of interconnectivity never before possible. This interconnectedness has made the world smaller and smaller.

During Labor Day weekend in 2014, President Obama commented on the collision between a troubled world and a smaller one. It had been a rough summer for the president and for world stability. Russia annexed Crimea and supported the separatist movement in Ukraine. ISIS captured Mosul, seized oil fields and banks, and slaughtered thousands of civilians while declaring a new caliphate. An Ebola outbreak in Africa reached pandemic levels with no containment in sight.

The president told a group of supporters: "The truth of the matter is that the world has always been messy. In part, we're just noticing now because of social media and our capacity to see in intimate detail the hardships that people are going through." Obama also noted that we faced greater challenges during the Cold War and we got through them. But during the Cold War there was no Twitter or Facebook to shape our interconnectedness.

In 500 years of communications history, only four major milestones occurred before the birth of the internet. Johannes Gutenberg's movable type in 1440, the advent of the telegraph and telephone, recorded media (voice and images), and finally, broadcast media (radio and television).

Clay Shirky spoke about the inherent flaw in these old modes of communication during a conference at the U.S. State Department. "The media that is good at creating conversations is no good at creating groups," he told those at the gathering. "And the media that is good at creating groups is no good at creating conversations."

## THE CASCADE

Social media emerged at just the right moment in history. It created groups. It created conversations. It connected users.

During the opening decade of the 21st century, our world got smaller and smaller. But its problems became larger. The collision of these two disparate circumstances produced The Great Convergence.

The intersection of the more troubled world with the smaller one happened with stunning alignment.

Soon after the terror attacks of 9/11, accounts of the tragic events were being posted, edited, revised, and amended on social media's first and most powerful online encyclopedia. Wikipedia was founded earlier in 2001 and would soon become the go-to information source for millions of people. On September 11, the site was updated in real time by users, making it the first time a social media site's users reported on a major breaking news event.

In April 2003, large numbers of refugees begin pouring into Chad. They were escaping a little-known part of Sudan called Darfur, and they brought reports of genocide. That same month, thousands of users online escaped real life for a virtual community online, created by Linden Lab, called Second Life.

On May 1, 2003, President Bush made a dramatic landing aboard the USS *Abraham Lincoln* on a fixed-wing fighter plane to announce the end of major combat operations in Iraq. It would soon become known as the "Mission Accomplished" speech. Five days later the author of that speech, and everyone else for that matter, could update their professional profile pages on a new social network: LinkedIn.

In August that year, MySpace went live the same week a great blackout swept across the northeastern U.S., rendering the internet and cell phones useless for days. For those in this part of the country, it would mark the last time they were not connected en masse for an extended period of time.

On February 3, 2004, the CIA announced that contrary to prewar statements, there were no weapons of mass destruction in Iraq. The next day, while sitting in his dorm room at Harvard, Mark Zuckerberg launched Facebook.

The last week of December 2004 brought tragedy to Southeast Asia. A 9.3 magnitude earthquake created a monster tsunami that slammed into the shores of Thailand, India, Sri Lanka, and other nations, killing more than 186,000 people. Several months later users could view videos of the destruction—or videos on nearly any topic, for that matter—thanks to a new website called YouTube.

July 2006 saw thousands killed in Iraq in the battle with insurgents. In the middle of that trying month, Twitter was released to the public. Users sent 224 tweets that first day, now the equivalent of one-tenth of one second of all daily tweets.

On October 6, 2010, a U.S. drone attack in North Waziristan, Pakistan, killed 11 suspected militants. That same day Instagram officially launched.

And on and on it went. The troubled world and the smaller one continued their collision. The Great Convergence happened in real time.

The Great Convergence changed our sense of geography, community, and responsibility. Problems were no longer "over there" in some far away land. Now, there was no such thing. Our collective triumphs and tragedies were all within reach. The Great Convergence made it easy for groups of like-minded people to band together. A sense of action took hold. It brought people closer in a world gone off the rails.

This zeitgeist shift opened the door for a new conversation. The world was in trouble. This was not a time for business as usual. It took The Great Convergence to bring this conversation to the forefront. Now it is here.

The Great Convergence opened the door to a new era: the era of social entrepreneurship.

It was in this environment that a transformative recipe for change took shape. The confluence of independent factors—a troubled world and a shrinking one—rewrote the rules for how society lives, works, and plays.

Social entrepreneurship is a model that is changing the world. It aims to fix the most entrenched problems facing mankind while building a successful and profitable business for its owners. This model challenges traditional definitions of success. It flies in the face of conventional thinking. It relies on technology and social media to thrive. Anyone can be a part of this movement. Its implications are far reaching for both the for-profit and nonprofit worlds. The Great Convergence explains the *why* behind social entrepreneurship's growth.

Burdened with debt, impotent to change, and beholden to special interests, government doesn't have the moxie to lead global change. The solutions now must come from elsewhere.

Social entrepreneurs are filling that void. And they can do it because of The Great Convergence.

Technology changed *how* social movements organize and coalesce. The Great Convergence changed what those issues were. Before The Great Convergence it was about you, your rights, your liberties, and your freedom. But after, it became something different. It became about us.

## MORE THAN A DREAM

On August 28, 1963, more than 2,000 buses rumbled into Washington, DC, along with trains, planes, and other vehicles packed with people from all over the country. Unsure how many people would arrive, the event organizers hoped for a turnout of 100,000. At 7:00 A.M., radio reporter David Eckelston reported ten people had gathered by the Lincoln Memorial. Organizers worried that the event would be a bust. But soon after, throngs of people appeared, and the March on Washington became the largest such gathering up to that time, with more than 250,000 people in attendance. That afternoon they heard the thunderous words of civil rights leaders, including Martin Luther King Jr. and John Lewis. The now famous speeches, along with the march itself, have been etched into history. But how did they do it?

No email. No Facebook. No Twitter. No SMS (because there were no cell phones). They didn't even have fax machines. All they had was a manual created by the brilliant March on Washington head organizer, Bayard Rustin. Rustin's 12-page booklet, *Final Plans for the March on Washington for Jobs and Freedom*, contained everything an attendee would need, from where to park and what to pack to where to use the bathroom. On the final page, an RSVP asked how many trains, buses, planes, or cars attendee groups planned to use and how many people they expected to come. It needed to be returned by mail. If there were any emergencies on the day of the march, it provided a phone number the captain of each bus, train, or plane should call.

They came for many reasons. Although he lacked a clear pathway to its passage, President Kennedy announced in June he would present a civil rights bill to Congress. Much of the South was still governed by Jim Crow laws that segregated bathrooms, drinking fountains, public places, and public transportation (nine years after *Brown v. Board of Education*, the South was still very much a segregated society). Earlier that summer in Birmingham, Bull Connor used hoses and attack dogs on peaceful protestors, which ignited a firestorm.

"I came because we want our freedom," Percy Lee Atkin of Clarksdale, Mississippi, told a reporter at the march. "What's it going to take to have your freedom?"

Estimates reported more than 60,000 of those who attended were white. The passage of a civil rights bill concerned many of them, too.

Radio reporter Arnold Shaw, who reported all day from the Lincoln Memorial, said, "One woman from San Diego, California, showed us her plane ticket. She said her grandfather sold slaves and she was here 'to help wipe out evil.'"

Civil rights was *the* social issue of the time. Directly or indirectly, the stain of racism touched every person who attended the march. With passions aflame and tensions high from a summer of violence— Medgar Evers had been shot and killed in Jackson, Mississippi, in early July—it's easy to understand why people were motivated to take action. One hundred years after President Lincoln signed the Emancipation Proclamation, black citizens were done waiting for change. They demanded it now.

It was a complicated endeavor. Imagine getting thousands of people to show up at the same location to support the fight against extreme poverty—an important issue no doubt, yet it pales in comparison to the visceral fight for civil rights in 1963. Everyone who attended the 1963 rally had been impacted one way or another by the civil rights movement. Why would people attend a rally to address poverty in the developing world? Unlike the March on Washington, none of the attendees would be the direct beneficiaries of the change they sought.

The Great Convergence did not create the ability for people to come together for a common cause. But it did change what that common cause could be. Victimhood of injustice was no longer a prerequisite for activism. It turns out knowledge of injustice— agnostic of its setting—could be the spark to action for today's generation.

Social entrepreneurs of today stand on the shoulders of civil rights leaders. The two movements share much in common. Fighting injustice and inequality, changing the course of history, their bonds run deep. Many social entrepreneurs use the civil rights activism of the 1960s as their North Star. It should be no surprise, then, that the tools and techniques used in that era have been co-opted and rebooted by social entrepreneurs.

## SOCIAL ENTREPRENEURS AS GLOBAL CITIZENS

Today's mass-event organizers can tap into The Great Convergence to bring people together on a scale never before possible. They can now attract citizens of the world—Global Citizens.

It started at 10:00 A.M.—precisely the time Bayard Rustin told attendees to arrive for the March on Washington. It was a balmy early spring day with temperatures reaching 83 degrees—the same high temperature recorded on August 28, 1963. And just like at the March on Washington, 250,000 people flooded the National Mall for a special call to action.

But on this April Day the crowd had assembled for a very different reason. People gathered to take action against extreme poverty and climate change. While none of the paid attendees were in extreme poverty, they all demanded a solution. The Global Poverty Project teamed up with the Earth Day Network as the organizing forces behind the event. They created a festive atmosphere for the occasion. To maximize their impact, they replaced the speeches of 1963 with music of today.

Why music? Global Poverty Project, the nonprofit organizer behind this and other similar events, addresses this on its website: "We believe that music transcends boundaries and languages and serves as an outlet for raising awareness around the issues that face everyone. Through music, we have an opportunity to reach millions with the message that we can end extreme poverty by 2030, end climate change, and give people like you the opportunity to take action on issues like ending preventable diseases, cutting carbon emissions, getting kids a better education, and ensuring everyone has safe access to toilets."

Top entertainers—Usher, Mary J. Blige, Train, Chris Martin, will.i.am, No Doubt, and others—took to the stage. They didn't just perform, they used their microphone as a soapbox.

"To end poverty, it starts, in my opinion, with an education about it," Usher told the crowd. "I want you to go and investigate for yourself so that you can really understand what's going on."

He went even further in an interview with the Associated Press. "I felt really good that the issues we are addressing here are on the table," he said. "Global warming is something that obviously will affect all of us. Clean water and sanitation is something that is very real. I understand and cannot turn a blind eye to what's going on."

One of the festival's hosts, will.i.am, said he believed it would be a catalyst, just like the 1963 March on Washington. "What I hope happens post the concert is that people go out and talk about some of the issues that we were spelling out today," he said. "Talk about solutions, go online, dig deep, and hold our leaders accountable for some of the things that they're pledging."

This festival has its own Bayard Rustin. His name is Hugh Evans, and at only 32 years old, he's changing the world. The Australian-born cofounder and CEO of the Global Poverty Project (which runs the Global Citizen Festival) is determined to bring about the end of extreme poverty by 2030. Working on issues ranging from water and sanitation to health, education, environment, hunger, finance, and innovation, the Global Poverty Project has leveraged more than $16 billion and received over 30 policy commitments from world leaders. Unlike Rustin, Evans can use numerous tools to connect with a community of like-minded people. With more than 145,000 followers on Twitter and over 721,000 followers on Facebook, it isn't hard for Evans and Global Citizen to rustle up a crowd.

Evans taps into The Great Convergence and rallies those who are tired of talk without action. What he has found is that people— particularly young people—care about ending extreme poverty.

Each fall Evans' organization hosts the Global Citizen Festival on the Great Lawn in Central Park. With the skyline of New York City as a backdrop, more than 60,000 people pack the lawn to hear musical performances and to learn how to end poverty. But there's more to it than that. Getting a ticket to the event requires, for most, more than just purchasing a ticket.

"We'd always conceived of a global citizen as being somebody that believes that extreme poverty is unjust and not something that should be a reality in our world. But the evolution of Global Citizen as a platform and the Global Poverty Project as an organization has been really interesting," Evans told a reporter before the 2015 Global Citizen Festival. "With the Global Citizen Festival, we decided we'd take the concept of the traditional charity concert and flip it on its head. So rather than charging people to attend an event and raising money, we came up with this idea that people use their voice, they participate in some way, shape, or form, before coming to the festival. Taking action is really their entry into the festival."

Evans adopted a gamification model of attendance. By registering on the Global Citizen website and taking an action—which can run the gamut from social media posts to volunteering—users earn points. When users reach enough points, they can secure a ticket to the festival. While some tickets are also available for sale, the majority of people who attend have earned their ticket through their advocacy work with the Global Poverty Project.

"With concerts like Live Aid or Live Earth, people would pay $120 for a ticket, and that would be their investment in the cause," Evans said. "What used to happen is on the night [of the concert], people would share these goals—let's get the G8 leaders to make a massive commitment around debt relief—which is fantastic, there's nothing wrong with that, but wouldn't it be awesome if you could use the whole period in the lead-up to the concert to [convey] that message?"

For the 2015 festival there was a push by Evans and his team to make potential attendees go the extra mile. The action steps they needed to take weren't easy. They weren't supposed to be easy. They took time, energy, and effort. There were calls to members of Congress, letters to the State Department, and other steps designed to spur action against global poverty.

"Music has a catalytic role in our culture—it has always been a fire starter," said Michele Anthony, executive vice president at Universal Music, who is involved in the Global Citizen Festival. "There are kids who are initially on [the site] because they couldn't get two tickets to a tour that was sold out. But the feedback that we're getting is that even kids who may not be that politically inclined are learning. They're getting engaged."

Evidence of The Great Convergence was vividly on display during the September 2015 Global Citizen Festival. The gates opened at 2:00 P.M., hours before the first act was set to play. By 3:45 P.M. the admission line stretched from 72nd Street in Manhattan down Central Park West to Columbus Circle. From there the line swung to the East Side, going all the way to the Plaza Hotel. The crowd, primarily Millennials, waited patiently as the line meandered slower than Manhattan rush hour traffic. Eventually attendees filed past security and onto the Great Lawn, where a massive crowd had already gathered.

I met a 20-something Millennial while the line made its way up to the Great Lawn. "It was a lot of work to earn this ticket, but it was worth it," she told me. "Sure, I get to attend this awesome concert, but I also did some good in the process."

It had been a busy 24 hours for Central Park. Just a day before, 80,000 people lined up to catch a glimpse of Pope Francis. While at the United Nations, the Pope made a call to action. The next day, he got it.

Leonardo DiCaprio. Bill and Melinda Gates. Ed Sheeran. Professor Jeffrey Sachs. Beyoncé. Michelle Obama. Coldplay. Malala Yousafzai. Pearl Jam. They were all present. The stars of the music and entertainment world collided with the stars of global development and progress.

There was world-class music and world-renowned speakers. There were videos on the UN's 17 Global Goals, which are part of the overarching effort to end extreme poverty, reduce income inequality, and prevent climate change.

Evans told *Billboard* magazine that 2 million global actions were taken during the festival. As one music executive put it, "For [attendees] to be involved in helping to effect change daily, that speaks to a different form of activism than perhaps this generation has seen— and that we haven't seen in a long time."

Eddie Vedder and Beyoncé teamed up for an acoustic version of Bob Marley's "Redemption Song" while a Nelson Mandela speech on humanity and overcoming poverty played along.

Michelle Obama appeared on video to highlight the *Let Girls Learn* initiative and then later arrived on the stage to introduce Beyoncé. Vice President Biden gave a rousing speech that seemed to best capture the spirit of the night.

"We have to move beyond, reach beyond, ourselves. We have to be a light to the world, not just in the world. That is what you are all here for tonight," Biden told the crowd. "I look out and I see lots of global citizens—optimistic, determined, absolutely determined, rejecting the false premise that our challenges are mere fate, with no solutions, and that protecting universal rights is equally universal, because it is."

What Biden looked out onto were Global Citizens eager to change a broken system. The zeitgeist shift, The Great Convergence, makes it possible to envision an entire reboot of capitalism in a way that lifts people up, solves problems, and promotes lasting change. It's called Capitalism 2.0, and its engine is social entrepreneurship.

# capitalism 2.0

*They always say time changes things,
but you actually have to
change them yourself.*

—Andy Warhol

19

American capitalism is a ferocious engine. Since being unleashed during the Industrial Revolution, America's economic output has been unprecedented. In the 40 years after the end of the Civil War, America had been transformed from a small-time primary producer into an emerging powerhouse. JPMorgan Chase calculated that by dawn of the 20th century, the United States could purchase the United Kingdom and settle its debt. Immigrants flooded our ports seeking a better life. Gilded or not, the perception around the world held that America was the place to be.

Government fueled the furnace for capitalism's engine. Whatever the challenge, government found a way to rise to the occasion. In 1939, our military was the 16th largest in the world, just behind Romania. By 1945, we were the mightiest nation in the history of mankind. We dammed rivers, built bridges, connected highways, sent men into orbit and then to the moon. We had a government that would meet any challenge, even a moonshot, "not because they are easy," President Kennedy said, "but because they are hard."

Capitalism clawed back from the Great Depression, when easy credit, speculation, and overleveraged positions had led to a dramatic collapse of the U.S. economy. The stock market did not fully recover from the 1929 crash until 1954. It took 25 years, a world war, the dawn of the Cold War, and a $50 billion New Deal, but capitalism persevered. It is of little wonder that the 20th century became known as the American Century. The title was well deserved.

Examples of America's largesse are everywhere. But no better place exemplifies our system than a supermarket.

## SUPERMARKETS: CAPITALISM BY THE AISLE

There is something uniquely American about supermarkets. The very first one opened on August 4, 1930, in Queens, New York. The Depression was getting worse by the month. But that didn't stop an American entrepreneur with a new idea. Michael Cullen launched King Kullen, and a new industry was born.

In their book on the expansive economic growth of the 20th century, Stephen Moore and Julian Simon wrote, "The affordability and availability of consumer goods have greatly increased. Even most poor Americans have a cornucopia of choices that a century ago the Rockefellers and the Vanderbilts could not have purchased."

The supermarket industry helped to create a vibrant middle class in America. Cheap prices allowed consumers to spread out their spending, and the economy grew further. President Kennedy honored the industry and noted its techniques ". . . have enabled a higher standard of living and have contributed importantly to our economic growth."

Supermarkets were more than just symbols of American might during the Cold War; they helped bring about its end. From 1958 to 1988, 50,000 Soviet citizens traveled to the United States. Upon entering an American supermarket they were aghast. Accustomed to one brand of coffee (usually poorly produced), they were agape at the choices of flavors and brands. And the food—it was everywhere.

Boris Yeltsin made the supermarket pilgrimage during a trip to Houston. After walking aisle after aisle, he noted: "When I saw those shelves crammed with hundreds, thousands of cans, cartons, and goods of every possible sort, for the first time I felt quite frankly sick with despair for the Soviet people. That such a potentially super-rich country as ours has been brought to a state of such poverty!"

Yes, supermarkets are a fine example of American capitalism and entrepreneurship.

They also are a lot like casinos. Both attempt to keep you there, spending your money, for as long as possible.

Have you ever wondered about the size of a shopping cart? It has nothing to do with convenience. Market research has demonstrated it is far bigger than the size needed for the average family. But it encourages you to keep filling it up.

Ever walk into a supermarket and wonder why the first things you see are fruits and vegetables? Yup, that's a marketing ploy as well. When people buy healthy food first, it makes them more likely to splurge on junk food later. They position flowers at the entrance, spread out staple foods, put milk in the back, all to get you to roam around and spend more money. Even the music is by design. Supermarkets aim to play music at a beat slower than the human heartbeat. This theoretically keeps you in the store longer and buying more goods. Yes, you can hear Celine Dion's music in both places.

Like casinos, supermarkets tend to be highly profitable ventures for their owners and shareholders. In 2014, U.S. supermarkets accumulated sales of $634 billion. That's roughly the annual GDP of Denmark and Egypt combined. Some of the richest people in the country come from this industry. Many have had their names enshrined on the Forbes 400. Capitalism has been good to them.

But that doesn't mean it has been good for everyone. Just like in a casino, when it comes to capitalism, there are those who beat the house and those who have their house taken from them.

The wealth has not been shared by all. Federal Reserve Chair Janet Yellen noted at a conference on income inequality: "By some estimates, income and wealth inequality are near their highest levels in the past hundred years, much higher than the average during that time span and probably higher than for much of American history before then."

While some supermarkets aim to pay a decent wage, many don't. Walmart has faced increasing criticism for its employee compensation packages. For a company that does $480 billion in annual sales, paying cashiers $8.81 per hour doesn't seem all that generous. In 2014, Walmart employees received $6.2 billion in welfare assistance from the federal government.

The environmental costs of supermarkets are enormous. Air freight may be tariff free, but it's also the most taxing mode of transportation per mile on the environment. The energy needed to refrigerate, heat, cool, and electrify supermarkets is staggering.

Supermarkets offer us a look into the strengths and shortcomings of capitalism.

Capitalism has driven innovation and change on a monumental scale. But its focus has been historically narrow. Its focus has been on profits. Economist Milton Friedman best summed up the role of business in 20th century society: "There is one and only one social responsibility of business—to use its resources and engage in activities designed to increase its profits," he wrote.

But what happens when things change? When the problems of the world compound on an epic scale? When the reach of government has been reduced? That's the world we find ourselves in today.

The public sector is mired in debt (now more than $18 trillion of it), inefficiency, and infighting. Government is handcuffed.

That is not to say government doesn't do anything. In fact, it does a lot. In 2013, the federal government shelled out $2,007,358,200,000 in entitlement and beneficiary money. Over half that went to Medicare and Social Security, the latter being one of the New Deal institutions which fueled the revival of American capitalism. As much as government can do, it also has its limits.

But here's the good news: Government doesn't need to go it alone. Now it has help. Capitalism 2.0 is coming to the rescue.

In a remarkable reboot, a new form of capitalism is changing the rules of business. It's tapping into America's entrepreneurial foundation, mixing it with a desire to make a difference, and wrapping it into a sound business practice. Profits and purpose were once in conflict with each other. The focus on one led to an erosion of the other, the thought went. That is no longer the case. Today, companies can earn a profit because they serve a larger purpose. Together with nonprofits they are changing the world and tackling problems that were once the domain of the public sector. Traditional boundaries have been blurred if not altogether scrapped. The results have been dramatic. The participants in this movement have fundamentally changed the world. And in this book you will discover how you can do it as well.

It's Capitalism 2.0: social entrepreneurship.

## SO, WHAT IS SOCIAL ENTREPRENEURSHIP?

If Capitalism 2.0 is a reboot of capitalism, then what precisely is social entrepreneurship? Ask three people to define it and you will get three different answers. There is no singular accepted definition of the field.

This isn't to suggest the movement is shrouded in mystery. There are accepted understandings of it. Social entrepreneurs are agents of change. Their reason for existing is to tackle problems confronting society.

So what's behind the lack of a definition? Entrepreneurship was defined more than 200 years ago. French economist Jean-Baptiste Say gave us what is still to this day a widely accepted definition. In his *Treatise on Political Economy* he wrote, "The entrepreneur shifts economic resources out of an area of lower and into an area of higher productivity and greater yield." The literal translation of "entrepreneur" from French into English is akin to "adventurer."

An adventurer seems a perfect way to describe an entrepreneur. Perhaps even a bit of a troublemaker. Someone who pushes boundaries and isn't afraid to take risks. Harvard Business School Professor Emeritus Abraham Zaleznik observed: "I think if we want to understand the entrepreneur, we should look at the juvenile delinquent."

Social entrepreneurship is a relatively new phenomenon. Without hundreds of years to establish a definition, and in a field that is constantly evolving, a universally accepted definition has been a moving target.

During the writing of this book, each of my interview subjects was asked for their own definition of social entrepreneurship. It turns out that was the hardest question for almost all of them.

"Social entrepreneurship exists in the space where the private sector won't go and government can't go," City University of New York Professor Thomas Lyons, an expert in the field, commented to me.

Writing in the *Stanford Social Innovation Review* a decade ago, New York University professor Paul C. Light gave a definition that I feel perfectly describes the term. "A social entrepreneur," he wrote, "is an individual, group, network, organization, or alliance of organizations that seeks sustainable, large-scale change through pattern-breaking ideas in what or how governments, nonprofits, and businesses do to address significant social problems."

I like to define social entrepreneurship broadly as the mechanism by which private sector actors solve public and private sector problems that are currently not being addressed.

Traditional entrepreneurs look for opportunities in new markets. So do social entrepreneurs. Traditional entrepreneurs need to return capital to investors. So do social entrepreneurs (albeit in differing structures that we'll examine later in this book). Traditional entrepreneurs require scale. So do social entrepreneurs.

But there are differences between them as well. The key distinguisher is: *why*. An entrepreneur is in business to deliver a bottom-line profit for serving a market in a better or more efficient manner. Social entrepreneurs have a triple bottom line to consider: people, planet, and profit. They are not looking to solve an immediate problem. Instead they are looking for scalable wholesale change to the underlying condition that led to the problem. As Bill Drayton of social entrepreneur network Ashoka put it: "Social entrepreneurs are not content just to give a fish or teach how to fish. They will not rest until they have revolutionized the fishing industry."

If that sounds more difficult than being an entrepreneur, well, it is. Sally Osberg, president of the Skoll Foundation, an organization promoting social entrepreneurship, said it best when comparing the two. She likened it to Ginger Rogers, who so elegantly danced with Fred Astaire. "The social entrepreneur does all that the entrepreneur does: comes up with a game-changing idea, builds the venture, attracts the capital, builds the market, brings the beneficiaries into the fold," she said. "But he or she does it backwards and in high heels."

Within the social entrepreneurial community sits a schism that makes its definition elusive. On the one hand, there's the school of thought championed by 2006 Nobel Peace Prize winner Muhammad Yunus. He sees social business as a virtuous cycle where profits are reinvested back into helping lift more people out of poverty. He adopted this practice at the Grameen Bank back in 1974. Later in this book, we'll explore Yunus's remarkable work in this field.

On the other hand are social entrepreneurs who believe profit-driven businesses with self-sustaining models will deliver more benefits, more efficiently, and to a greater number of people. This schism was put on display in a 2006 *The New Yorker* article by Connie Bruck. Her "Millions for Millions" story centered on how to best get results in microfinance. But as it turns out, the debate was a microcosm of a larger one within the social entrepreneurial community. To this day the for-profit versus nonprofit debate remains heated. As you'll see in this book, there is an answer. They are both right. Yet they are both wrong.

If ever there was a need for a big tent, it's now. We need to encourage more people to enter social enterprise and to be embraced by the community of change. Even Capitalism 2.0 will have its limits. As several sources in this book said to me: Not every problem is a market. It would be overly simplistic to believe that the slate of global problems could be eradicated solely by market forces. For this reason, the big tent also includes nonprofits that fill a tremendously important space.

Despite the degree of difficulty in social entrepreneurship's practice and definition, more and more are flocking to the movement every day. Those who join in care less about its definition than they do about its impact. Social entrepreneurship connects with many on a very elemental level. Perhaps even on a holy one.

In the early rabbinic period of Judaism this connection was called Tikkun Olam, which translates to "heal the world." In the Gospel of Luke the story of the rich man and Lazarus reminds Christians of their responsibility to fix the problems of the world. The Qur'an describes the importance of charity and giving back in a Muslim's life (2:267).

Social entrepreneurship is not new. It has been with us since man became master over beasts of burden. What's new is the velocity in the movement and the attention it now receives. The volume of and the speed at which new ventures are being launched under the social entrepreneurial banner is staggering. But make no mistake about it: Social entrepreneurship has been with Americans since, well, one of the very first Americans.

Benjamin Franklin accomplished many firsts, from bifocals to the wood stove. He was the first American millionaire. He has gone down in history as the "first American." Franklin was also our first social entrepreneur.

# BEN FRANKLIN, SOCIAL ENTREPRENEUR

Franklin was a character. At age 70 he arrived in France to press for French intervention in the American Revolution. He appeared before the royal court dressed plainly. Franklin stood in stark contrast to the ornate Versailles court. Leaders of Paris first looked on with curiosity and bemusement at this new world figure. Soon enough, he was a hit with the aristocracy. His likeness was everywhere: on watches, medallions, and street signs. He even set fashion trends when the "coiffure a la Franklin" became a hit with the rich women of Paris, who wore furs atop their heads instead of the traditional wig. Franklin secured French involvement in the American Revolution and changed the course of history when the U.S. won the war.

A polymath, he made his mark in printing, publishing, science, and statesmanship. He's often referred to as the only president of the United States who wasn't president of the United Sates. With so much written about Franklin over the three centuries since his birth, it's hard to imagine a new way to look at Franklin. Until you consider that Franklin was America's first social entrepreneur.

In 1727, the 21-year-old Franklin founded a socially and civically minded organization called Junto. Gathered together for regular meetings were "like-minded aspiring artisans and tradesmen who hoped to improve themselves while they improved their community," noted Michael Mumford in his work on Franklin and social innovation.

Franklin never once took out a patent on any of his wonderful inventions. He preferred that the maximum number of people benefit from their service. In his autobiography he recalled his 1742 open stove invention. "Gov'r. Thomas was so pleas'd with the construction of this stove, as described in it, that he offered to give me a patent for the sole vending of them for a term of years; but I declin'd it from a principle which has ever weighed with me on such occasions, viz., That, as we enjoy great advantages from the inventions of others, we should be glad of an opportunity to serve others by any invention of ours; and this we should do freely and generously."

Like most of his pursuits, Franklin was ahead of his time. His foray into social entrepreneurship helped weave it into the fabric of American values. Franklin wasn't afraid of change and he certainly wasn't afraid to challenge the status quo.

## THEY'VE HAD IT

Today's social entrepreneurs take this same approach. The status quo has little meaning or significance to them. They are driven by a unique alchemy.

The Great Convergence shaped them. A zeal to repair the world, coupled with a frustration with the way things are, created a group of people who have just HAD IT.

They've HAD IT with problems that have gone unsolved.

They've HAD IT with models that have haven't yielded enough results.

They've HAD IT with naysayers who see no alternative to the world as it is.

Channeling their passion to make a difference, social entrepreneurs apply a HAD IT attitude: **H**ope, **A**udacity, **D**isappointment, **I**ngenuity, and **T**enacity. They've HAD IT and therefore are poised to make a difference.

### *Hope*

Social entrepreneurs are arguably one of the most hopeful groups of people you will ever encounter. Problem solving is hard. Harder still is to solve the underlying issues that lead to those problems in the first place. Their ultimate goal is to put themselves out of business by creating a world without poverty, with equal access to health care and education, gender and racial parity, and a protected, natural environment.

David Bornstein, noted authority in the field, commented that "social entrepreneurs have the hope, vision, and power to change the world."

## *Audacity*

"We got this," superstar Millennial Maggie Doyne told me. Doyne wasn't just referring to her incredible charity based in Nepal (that you'll read about later in this book). She was referring to the global problems facing us today—all of them. This same level of audacity runs through the veins of all social entrepreneurs. They dispel the notion that some problems are intractable.

It takes a certain level of audaciousness to believe you can have scalable impact on not just thousands but potentially millions of people. Several social entrepreneurs you will read about in this book told me their goal was to touch more than 100 million lives.

## *Disappointment*

Pick your poison: the environment, poverty, human trafficking, public health, education, water, food. The list goes on and on. Social entrepreneurs have inherited a world not of their creation and not of their design. Venture capitalist John Doerr began his remarkable TED Talk on clean energy with a story about his teenage daughter. She was disappointed in those in her father's generation. She believed they caused global warming and thus they needed to fix it. An emotional Doerr pleaded with the audience to tackle climate change so he could "look forward to the conversation" he would have with his daughter in 20 years.

There's a level of sadness social entrepreneurs experience. They can't believe these problems have gone on without an effective solution. Like any athlete knows, disappointment can hold you back or it can motivate you to work harder. The key for social entrepreneurs is to channel that disappointment to fuel positive social change.

## *Ingenuity*

The approach of the social entrepreneur is new. It requires challenging the status quo. Instead of looking to the poor as a group to be pitied, social entrepreneurs view them as a market where goods and services can benefit both parties. Any successful product made by a social entrepreneur is either disruptive or innovative, or, perhaps, both. When selling a product in the developing world, it's very possible that no competition exists. Such was the case when d.light began selling its solar lights in 2008.

"Fundamentally, if it wasn't us, someone else probably would have done it. We are in the perfect market," d.light cofounder Sam Goldman told me. "There was this crazy market failure going on with this crappy technology called kerosene that was super expensive. We had this amazing convergence of first, solar prices dropping and LED prices dropping—nothing to do with us. Battery prices came down, too. We had this technology convergence happen for totally separate reasons, exactly at the time that the social enterprise space exploded."

In the developed world where consumers tend to have choices, social entrepreneurs need to disrupt existing models. From healthy food choices to better educational and vocational opportunities, social entrepreneurs take ingenuity to a whole new level.

### *Tenacity*

Social entrepreneurs tackle problems that have a high degree of difficulty. To mount a proper charge against large obstacles it takes a certain attitude and mindset. It takes tenacity to the tenth degree.

"This is hard work," said Goldman. "If you are going to leverage your time, your relationships, your sweat, your money into solving a problem, why not try to solve problems that if you are successful in, you move history in the right direction?"

NYU professor Paul Light once said: "I also find that social entrepreneurs are driven by a persistent, almost unshakable optimism. They persevere in large part because they truly believe that they will succeed in spite of messages to the contrary."

## THE TIPPING POINT

That's the power of Capitalism 2.0. It reaches into new and undiscovered markets. It pushes organizations to think anew. It empowers those across the economic spectrum.

Capitalism 2.0 is taking traditional capitalists out of their comfort zone. It poses this question: How can our company succeed and at the same time tackle the world's toughest problems? Social entrepreneurs' problem-solving approach fits perfectly today. It doesn't focus on those drops in the bucket. It expands the bucket, making it bigger, stronger, and more sustainable.

"This is the tipping point, the first time in the history of capitalism where it is OK for businesses to engage with poverty. It is not bad to help and make money," Ranjit Voola, a professor at the University of Sydney, recently told *Business Insider*.

Similarly, Apple CEO Tim Cook told attendees of a recent software conference: "Business has a very important responsibility to society. That responsibility has grown markedly in the last couple of decades or so as government has found it more difficult to move forward."

The direction and momentum of Capitalism 2.0 is so strong that it might one day remove the qualifier "social" from social entrepreneur. All entrepreneurs—in fact, all businesses—may morph into entities that act like social entrepreneurs. "In the future," Soushiant Zanganehpour, a thought leader in social entrepreneurship, said, "we expect the fundamental values of social entrepreneurship to become incorporated into mainstream business practice." Some will come to embrace this. Other entities will see it as a threat. If the tailwinds become strong enough, there will be no stopping this evolution of business.

And when it comes together—when businesses act like Professor Voola suggests, how Tim Cook describes, and how Zanganehpour envisions—what does it look like? It looks a lot like Judith Joan Walker of African Clean Energy.

## ACING THE CHALLENGE

One person dies every eight seconds from illnesses borne out of inhaling open flame cooking smoke. That is the equivalent of losing the entire population of New Zealand every single year. The hazards of open flame cooking in the developing world have been well documented for many years. The inhalation of smoke and black carbon can lead to lung disease, eye disease, and death. Since women and children tend to be the primary food preparers, they are the most at risk for such afflictions. Some 4.3 million people succumb annually to illnesses from open flame cooking, which is more than the amount of people who die from HIV/AIDS and malaria—combined.

The solution seems pretty straightforward. People should use an alternative stove that doesn't produce dangerous smoke. That approach has been tried many times. Charities have given them away. Typically they have been stoves designed for the developed world or cheaply made products that could be adapted for use in the developing world. Generally speaking, these products reduce smoke; they don't eliminate it. As a result, these stoves haven't been problem solving or game changing. Enter African Clean Energy (ACE) and its enigmatic COO and director of operations, Judith Joan Walker.

"There is a perception it will fail or crash and burn," Walker told me. "We are here to make this a sustainable business. It can be done in a different way."

How is the clean stovetop produced by ACE different? Walker explained that in the past, NGOs (non-governmental organizations) and nonprofits have offered low-quality products. ACE started with the premise that the poor are customers, and like any smart company, it starts with creating the right product for your customers. "No one says, 'Give me a shitty, cheap product'—that's not what they want. We don't treat the less fortunate like they are a lower class," Walker said. Instead, ACE treats them like a market filled with potential customers.

"Our customers—I want to treat them as customers. Let's stop treating poor people like they don't know what they want," she said. With this in mind, ACE has engineered a product for the poor's needs. First, it eliminates all smoke, rather than dampening it. Second, it works on multiple fuel sources, including biomass pellets and cow pies. Sensing my surprise, Walker went on to discuss the particulars of cow pies that make them an excellent fuel source. The stove gasifies the fuel source to create a smokeless burn, which eliminates the daily hazards faced by those who rely on open flame cooking.

The ACE-1, as the device is called, comes with a DC connector and USB port that can turn the product into a power source. This is perfect for powering lanterns and other electronic devices. It is more than a convenience—it is a necessity for many who live in areas that don't have access to an electricity grid. Microlending through M-Pesa and Kiva makes the device affordable to a larger share of the market. Default rates remain remarkably low.

The ACE-1 is made in Lesotho, a tiny, poor country surrounded by South Africa and not known for its manufacturing prowess. African Clean Energy is helping the local economy by creating jobs, which allows it to have a greater impact outside of its customer base.

The for-profit model is clearly different. It channels Capitalism 2.0 by bringing profits to ACE and helping the world at the same time. By reducing the number of people using open flame for cooking purposes, it presents tremendous upside for a more healthy community. That increases productivity in a powerful way. "The way we've done things before is like we are looking to alleviate our colonial guilt. We go in and hand out stuff and—'You aren't doing what we think you should be doing, so try this.'"

And because consumers—all consumers—like choices, the product comes in multiple colors. Walker gets asked the same question all the time: "Why aren't you a nonprofit?"

When I posed that same question to her, she was ready with her reply. "Because we are doing something good for the world, we should also do it for free—that's the strange perception of the world," Walker said. "If you are doing something good for the world, you shouldn't make money on it. Just like directors of NGOs or charities; they should not make money. But tomorrow if I designed an app that gave you funny eyebrows and it went crazy and everyone was sharing it and I made a billion dollars on an app that gave you a funny-looking face, everyone would pat me on the back and say congrats. But if you are doing something incredible, people are dubious."

African Clean Energy is scaling its model. It is raising investment capital, creating jobs, and building a strong, sustainable business. It is also creating a win-win. "We can do well financially and have no downside whatsoever," Walker said. "That's how the world should be."

## THINKING BIG

But what about the big picture? How has social entrepreneurship driven the markets to rethink their investments and the strategies behind them? Successful financial institutions respond very well to changes in the marketplace. Social entrepreneurs have created pioneering change. Now Wall Street can do what it does best: monetize those changes. Only in this space—impact investing—monetization has a binary impact: It is financial as well as social.

"The big debate during the 20th century was about the relationship between the market and the state. Both those institutions are now tarnished," *The New York Times* columnist David Brooks lamented. "The market is prone to devastating crashes and seems to be producing widening inequality. Government is gridlocked, sclerotic, or captured by special interests. Government is an ever more rigid and ineffective tool to address market failures." But Brooks was hopeful. He had recently been turned on to a new way to look at markets.

For as far back as anyone could remember, it went like this. Investments were divided into four general categories: speculative, capital appreciation, income, and capital preservation. For short-term and long-term investors, financial goals extended from low to high risk. The focus of that investment was singular: gaining capital. There was never a conversation about change or impact. When a liquidity event struck, and good fortune from a well-placed investment yielded a gain, it presented the investor with opportunities and options of what to do with the proceeds. One popular option was (and still is) charity.

Charity was the afterthought. It's what you did after making money. The Puritans would have been proud: 385 years after John Winthrop laid out his vision for charity in the new world, it still held to form. Until now.

# INVESTING WITH IMPACT

Social entrepreneurship has put forth a new paradigm for thinking about making money and driving change. In this new archetype both happen hand in hand. It doesn't involve post-liquidity giving; in fact it doesn't involve giving at all. Instead it's a new way of investing. There is a market for change making. Like any other market it can produce profits for its investors. Impact investing is a driving force behind Capitalism 2.0.

"Investors are increasingly rejecting the notion that they face a binary choice between investing for maximum risk-adjusted financial return or donating money to social and environmental causes," Robert Ruttman of Credit Suisse wrote in a report jointly issued by the bank and the World Economic Forum. "These impact investors are proactively using their investments to generate a tangible social or environmental impact, while also having the potential for some financial return."

Impact investing is not only limited to the for-profit space. Nonprofits have been a dynamic force in impact investing. Instead of relying on the donor treadmill for continuous funding, impact investing gives them a newfound revenue stream. With the proceeds from a successful impact investment, the nonprofit gains the wherewithal to reinvest in other ventures without relying on donors to fund it.

There are three central characteristics to impact investing:

1. *The Intent.* The investor risks capital with the expectation of producing a social impact. This is different from other investments that could have latent or unintended beneficial implications for society. Here it is central to the investment itself.
2. *The Return on Investment.* A financial return is expected through a social impact investment. What happens with that return depends on the structure of the company responsible for its implementation. A for-profit firm will be rewarded with a profit for itself, fellow investors, or clients. This return can run the spectrum from speculative to capital preservation (also known as a concessionary return). It is no different in principle from

the return expectations that come with traditional investing. Nonprofits, as described earlier, would roll the capital into a future investment. This provides them with fresh investment capital without relying on a donor base for funds.

3. *The Impact.* Investors have grown accustomed to measuring their investments by the amount of returns they deliver. With impact investing there is another, crucial metric: the social impact it delivers.

Investors have been pleased with the financial and social returns on their impact investments. In a recent survey by the Global Impact Investing Network (GIIN), 91 percent of respondents discovered their financial returns were in line with or exceeded their initial hopes, while 98 percent found their social impact was in line with or higher than expected.

GIIN got started in 2007, with assistance from the Rockefeller Foundation, as early investors were looking to better understand the principles behind impact investing. Since 2009, GIIN has built market infrastructure and supports research, education, and activities of the impact investing community.

As with any investment, success breeds more interest, and subsequently more capital flows into it. Now more than 2,000 of GIIN's members subscribe to ImpactBase, its online directory of impact investment funds and products. An annual survey of 146 large impact investors by GIIN and JPMorgan Chase found the investors had committed $10.6 billion to impact investments in 2014. But GIIN has much bigger aspirations for the sector. If impact investing could account for just 1 percent of all global financial assets, it would equal $2 trillion.

To complement GIIN, a series of common metrics for reporting the performance of impact capital was created. Investors needed the ability to make fair comparisons among different impact investing opportunities. The comparisons weren't just about financial return; investors also wanted to know about social and environmental impact. In 2011, some 29 organizations signed a letter of support for the

Impact Reporting and Investment Standards (IRIS) initiative. It was a powerful coalition of for-profit and nonprofit entities joining to support this framework for standardized social and environmental performance reporting. When coupled with the Global Impact Investing Rating System (GIIRS, pronounced "gears"), a dynamic online system that reviews impact assessment of companies and funds akin to Morningstar, IRIS gives investors a clear and concise impact overview.

With a standardized system in place to measure performance, the impact investment community continues to become mainstream. Since 2008, the global community of social impact investors has descended on the annual SOCAP (Social Capital Markets) conference, which bills itself as the intersection of money and meaning. More than 2,000 people attend this perennially sold out event, which is dedicated to accelerating the market for impact investing. Originally founded by MissionHUB, an impact hub of co-working spaces for change makers, the conference has positioned itself at the very heart of the impact investment movement.

The list of featured speakers from the 2015 event shows how intertwined the world of impact investing has become with capital markets. Bill Drayton of Ashoka, Deborah Winshel of BlackRock, Cheryl Dorsey of Echoing Green, and Deval Patrick of Bain Capital (and former governor of Massachusetts) were just a few of the big names that addressed the large audience.

Fran Seegull, chief investment officer and managing director of ImpactAssets, shared her belief ahead of the 2015 conference that mainstreaming of impact investing had truly come of age. According to Seegull, there has been a 76 percent growth in dollars allocated to impact investment over the past three years. Goldman Sachs, JPMorgan Chase, Morgan Stanley, BNY Mellon, and Merrill Lynch are now actively working in the space, she noted. These institutional clients are working with wealthy individuals, pension funds, foundations, and endowments, all of which are seeing the benefits of impact investing. But just like the broader investing universe, are the direct financial benefits limited to the 1 percent?

Seegull says no. She notes that deposit assets at several community banks, ESG-screened mutual funds, and maybe the biggest door opener of them all, crowdfunding, should give nonaccredited investors opportunities. "The democratization of impact investing is something that I am very interested in and is poised to transform impact investing," she wrote.

No wonder that in his *The New York Times* article on the topic, Brooks noted, "Someday government will get unstuck, with new programs to address this new era. But there's no prospect of that happening soon. Right now social capitalism is a more creative and dynamic place to spend a life."

## B DIFFERENT

Two new corporate designations should help further Capitalism 2.0: Certified B Corps and benefit corporations. Both are designed to galvanize the Business of Good community and further its goals.

The concept of a B corporation was developed in 2006 by Jay Coen Gilbert, Bart Houlahan, and Andrew Kassoy. Gilbert and Houlahan had made their mark in business with AND1, a basketball shoe company known for its basketball mix tapes and edgy footwear. In a market dominated by big players like Nike, AND1 rose from $4 million in revenue in 1995 to over $250 million by 2001. After the company was sold, its cofounders explored several options for what to do next. They knew they wanted to be involved with work that had meaning, and they wanted to use their passion for good.

The idea behind B Corps is that capitalism needs to move from shareholder capitalism to stakeholder capitalism. It's about creating value for shareholders while also creating value for society, Gilbert, cofounder of the nonprofit B Lab, said during his 2010 TEDx talk.

See the full Jay Coen Gilbert TEDx talk at
https://www.youtube.com/watch?v=mGnz-w9p5FU

## WHY BECOME A B CORP?

To achieve a shareholder to stakeholder shift, Jay Coen Gilbert and his partners wanted to create an infrastructure and a calling card for those companies dedicated to the triple bottom line approach.

But why would a company want to be boxed in to the structure of a B Corp? It loses flexibility to iterate into a new line of business that may not fit within B Corp guidance. But what it gains is so much more. B Lab contends that, "By voluntarily meeting higher standards of transparency, accountability, and performance, Certified B Corps are distinguishing themselves in a cluttered marketplace by offering a positive vision of a better way to do business."

Companies across the country have received this message loud and clear. There are more than 1,200 registered B Corps today. Receiving this designation is not easy. It involves real compliance and review, unlike some other designations that require nothing more than a Mastercard or Visa. B Corps are evaluated using three key metrics: accountability, transparency, and performance. The certification fees range from $500 to $50,000 per year, depending on company revenues.

*Esquire* magazine summed up B Corps this way: "It might turn out to be like civil rights for blacks or voting rights for women—eccentric, unpopular ideas that hold and change the world."

Thanks to B Lab, the private sector has created a structure to evaluate corporate responsibility, governance, and performance. Government has finally taken notice and has developed critically important tools to support this sector as well.

On April 14, 2010, a second wave in this new approach to business took hold. With private sector tools in place, state governments climbed aboard the Business of Good caravan.

---

**WHY BECOME A B CORP?,** CONTINUED

In a remarkable sign of bipartisan appeal, the Maryland State Senate voted 44-0, followed soon after by its General Assembly, which voted 135-5, to ratify the bill before them: SB690, which established the first benefit corporation legislation in America. Maryland's governor, Martin O'Malley, quickly signed it into law.

Benefit corporation status is now available in 31 states. Unlike the certification achieved through a B Corp, a benefit corporation is a type of legal structure. It has a different set of standards and is not legally required to be audited, although it is sound business practice to do so. Each benefit corporation, however, must create a benefit report. This report is part of a rapidly growing online database used to measure performance of the company's social impact.

Many well-known companies have gone this route and are registered as benefit corporations, including Patagonia, Method, and Plum Organics.

Benefit corporate status gives clear notice to investors that the company is seeking social good as a competitive advantage and that the company will have the triple bottom line approach. By defining its purpose, a company can seek out consumers aligned with its vision while attracting like-minded investors. Some benefit corporations also seek B Corp status; however, there is no requirement to do so.

---

## THE POWER OF PATIENCE

Perhaps no organization has come to better represent the dynamism of social capital than Acumen. Founded in 2001 by the incomparable Jacqueline Novogratz, this nonprofit has harnessed Capitalism 2.0 to create a new model for investing. Markets and charity have their

---

**WHY BECOME A B CORP?,** CONTINUED

### B Corp versus Benefit Corporation

| Issue | B Corps | Benefit Corps |
|---|---|---|
| Accountability | All stakeholders need to be considered | Same |
| Transparency | Must publish reporting of performance measured against third-party standards | Same |
| Performance | Required to accrue a minimum score on B Impact Assessment | Self-Reporting |
| Availability | Available to any U.S. corporation | Available in 31 states and DC |
| Cost | $500 to $50,000/year depending on revenue | State filing fees range from $70–$200 |

---

strengths and weaknesses. Markets generally require immediate returns to satisfy investors. Charities have limited ability to scale.

"Clearly, we're living in a moment of crisis. Arguably the financial markets have failed us and the aid system is failing us, and yet I stand firmly with the optimists who believe that there has probably never been a more exciting moment to be alive," Novogratz told attendees of TED@State, a TED gathering at the U.S. State Department.

Acumen is a response to the current debate about how to best alleviate global poverty. Is the answer more aid, or is the problem better served by capital markets? To Acumen these aren't mutually exclusive. Both sides of this debate can point to successes. As a result, it has developed the philosophy of "patient capital." When Acumen invests in a social enterprise, the exit from that venture is typically seven to ten years. In today's world of frenetic markets and laser focus on short-term quarterly performance, that time horizon certainly qualifies as patient. Acumen investments are made in the form of debt or equity and range from $250,000 to $3 million.

"Patient capital works between, and tries to take the best of both," Novogratz said. "It's money that's invested in entrepreneurs who know their communities and are building solutions to health care, water, housing, and alternative energy, thinking of low-income people not as passive recipients of charity, but as individual customers, consumers, clients, people who want to make decisions in their own lives."

To fund the investments, Acumen creates a virtuous cycle. It begins with charitable donations. The money received will not be paid back but will be deployed as an investment vehicle. After the investment is made and the company has grown to create game-changing social impact through scale, the investment is reinvested. That money is then recycled for future investments. As Acumen builds successful companies, its ability to invest in other social enterprises grows.

Acumen is agnostic on the organizational structures of its portfolio companies. Both for-profits and nonprofits are eligible for investment capital; however, nonprofits must have a revenue-generating activity so the organization can be financially sustainable. Nonprofits are held to the same standards as for-profits in that a return to Acumen is expected.

Here's what Acumen looks for in a portfolio company. Geography is a key criterion for investment; Acumen seeks companies with operations in East Africa, West Africa, India, Pakistan, or Latin America. Acumen works in six investment sectors: education, energy, health, housing, agriculture, and water. It looks for early to mid-stage companies that have begun the process of scaling. This means newly minted startups are outside its general framework. Investees must have businesses that can scale, develop a sustainable financial entity, and of course have significant social impact.

Since its inception Acumen has made a demonstrable impact on the world. It has invested north of $88 million in more than 82 companies. These investments have touched 100 million people and created more than 60,000 jobs. Consider all it did with $88 million versus the $50 billion in annual foreign aid doled out by the U.S. government.

Acumen has invested in ambulances in Mumbai, mobile platforms for farmers in Ghana, solar home systems in Uganda, sustainable sanitation in Kenya, affordable drip irrigation in Pakistan, and locally produced anti-malaria bed nets in Tanzania.

In her wonderful book, *The Blue Sweater*, Novogratz stated, "We've seen what can happen when an entrepreneur views the market as a listening device that reveals how to tailor services and products to the preferences of low-income people who are viewed as consumers, not victims." By using the virtue of patience and the power of markets, Acumen has demonstrated a new way forward to solving the problem of poverty.

## BEING UNREASONABLE

Social entrepreneurs are revolutionizing old and new markets, altering the landscape of charity, and disrupting everything we thought we knew about business. Who are social entrepreneurs anyway?

The Great Convergence has shaped them all. They've been spurred to action by some experience with an unjust world. That experience could be tangential through social media or experienced firsthand. "This is worthy of my life's work," one of them told me.

And if you've got what it takes, maybe you can be *unreasonable*. It's what Daniel Epstein has been for his entire career.

Epstein is the founder and chief protagonist of the Unreasonable Group. It's a collection of ventures that includes a startup institute, incubator, accelerator, venture capital, production company, and a blog and video portal, all under the Unreasonable banner. This network of mostly for-profit ventures is tethered to the belief that the biggest challenges facing us today can all be solved through social entrepreneurship.

It takes collaborators to make Capitalism 2.0 work. That's what Unreasonable does. At the Unreasonable Institute, they throw social entrepreneurs together for five days to five weeks at a time for sessions that are part business boot camp, part motivational, and part aspirational. Social ventures apply, looking to leverage the

Unreasonable network, which includes mentors and experts in scaling, fundraising, business plan development, executive coaching, and more.

Originally Unreasonable charged an upfront cost to attend, but now ventures take part in a revenue share agreement that comes with a money-back guarantee. Even nonprofits can partake through various other means.

Getting into the Unreasonable Institute isn't easy. Each year there are more applicants. As the network of alumni grow, so, too, does the prestige of the Institute. The alumni network now spans more than 50 countries. All companies must possess a common denominator for enrollment: Their idea needs to be scalable to impact 1 million people. That means only the most audacious social entrepreneurs who are dead set on making large and lasting impacts are a part of the Unreasonable family.

Epstein tells a story. There are two shoemakers. They set sail from London and go down to the Horn of Africa. There, they hear, there could be something. Their ship comes in. They leap off it and survey the scene. The first shoemaker dispatches immediately back to London, "This is a disaster. No one has shoes. This is the worst shoe market in the world," he declares. Then the other shoemaker reports back to London, "No one here has shoes," he says. "This is the biggest market opportunity in the world."

Epstein identifies with the second man in the story. "I'm a die-hard optimist. I was raised in a way to respect values more than rules," he said. So he broke a few rules, held true to his values and optimism, and created a vehicle to help social entrepreneurs soar.

Attendees and alumni are clearly enamored with the Unreasonable Institute. Two weeks into the first program, two entrepreneurs got tattoos with the Unreasonable logo—a light bulb with wings. This was symbolic, a reminder literally tattooed onto them that dreams can be realized even in the face of enormous skepticism. "People who go through the program are called unreasonable," Epstein said. "The tattoo reminds people that they are not alone." Since then the concept has taken off, and now 40 to 50 people, including Epstein, have the tattoo.

I was once at a cocktail reception for a social venture and overheard two people talking about how to make social entrepreneurship grow. The conversation soon turned to Epstein. "Daniel Epstein is the man," one declared, pumping his fist for emphasis.

Hard to disagree with that.

# CHAPTER THREE

# challenging the charity industrial complex

*Behold I do not give lectures*
*or a little charity,*
*When I give*
*I give myself.*

— WALT WHITMAN

O n a beautiful fall evening in 2015, about a hundred guests gather at the lower level bar of the Crosby Street Hotel in New York City. An hour before the formal presentation, guests mingle while sipping cocktails and eating canapés. The guests are a mix of young urban professionals in finance, real estate, venture capital, private equity, and the nonprofit world. For many this is their first time attending an event hosted by this organization. Little do they know it, but they are about to get the full Scott Harrison.

Tall and elegant with salt and pepper hair and piercing eyes, it's hard to miss Harrison when he's present in any room. Two doors adjacent to the bar suddenly swing open and reveal a screening room. The guests slowly make their way to their seats. Harrison greets many of them personally. He then strides to the front of the room, struts up four steps, and stands in front of the crowd. He's briefly introduced, and then, with a 30-by-12-foot screen behind him, he begins. It is now slightly after 7:30 P.M. For the next 70 minutes he will speak, uninterrupted, to a mesmerized audience.

Harrison begins with a personal story. The audience learns about his life growing up in Philadelphia. His mother was exposed to carbon monoxide and it wreaked havoc on her immune system, leaving her deeply ill. Harrison first arrived in New York City as a freshman at NYU. There he worked as a party promoter, making more money than he could imagine. Harrison was a good party promoter, a really good one. Corporate sponsors paid him to be seen in public drinking their alcoholic beverage. He shows the audience a slide of him seated in a VIP section with a big, fat Rolex watch on his wrist. "And yes," he confesses to the audience, "I wanted people to see me with that watch."

He was in the fast lane with a fast crowd. Excessive drinking, illegal drugs—they all came with the territory, and Harrison eagerly embraced it. "I was selling selfishness and decadence," he tells the audience. "I was the worst person I knew." By 2004, Harrison grew despondent about his life's work and the choices he had made. He wanted to reconnect with his Christian faith and find new purpose in life. He signed up as a volunteer for Mercy Ships, a humanitarian aid organization that brings in doctors and health-care professionals to treat those in the developing world who lack such access. Harrison brought with him a camera and an open mind.

He warns the audience that the pictures are not easy to see, but important. Images of people with gargantuan tumors, cleft palates, and faces destroyed by flesh-eating amoebae appear in rapid-fire succession. There is some good news. The audience then sees the post-surgical pictures displaying the help many of these people received. "Over the next eight months, I met patients who taught me the meaning of courage," he recalls. "Many of them had been slowly suffocating to death for years and yet pressing on, praying, hoping, surviving. It was an honor to photograph them. It was an honor to know them."

On his second mission with Mercy Ships, Harrison learned one of the things making these people sick was dirty water. Local villagers drank water from ponds because they had no other water source. He also saw what happened to a community when a clean-water source was installed. It was a profoundly moving experience for him.

A few years later, on his 31st birthday, Harrison launched charity: water. He was good at throwing parties and he had a list of names "about 15,000 long," he says. So he threw a different kind of party. He charged $20 for admission to his birthday party at Tenjune. That night he raised $15,000, and his nonprofit's commitment to supplying clean, safe drinking water to those in the developing world was born.

Explaining the clean-water crisis is not easy. Most people don't even know there is a crisis in the first place, and others have trouble understanding its size. "A water crisis for my friends is a $10 bottle of Pellegrino," Harrison jokes.

So Harrison set his sights high in starting his own charity. "I wanted to reinvent giving," he tells the audience. "I tried to get friends involved, but they thought charities were just big black holes. I give my money. I don't know where it goes. Everyone seemed to have horror stories." And there's where Harrison saw opportunity.

He opened not one bank account but two—one dedicated to field work and the other for operations. One hundred dollars was deposited in each. The idea was surprisingly simple: "We could say every time 100 percent of your money could go into the field," he says. The overhead costs would be covered by a second set of donors who understood their funds in this account would not go into the field.

This is the inverse of how we've come to understand giving. The established norm was to keep overhead at a minimum and direct as much firepower as possible to the field. But Harrison wanted to tell stories. He didn't want to regurgitate statistics. He didn't want to do bulk mail campaigns with long letters and sad pictures. "I really wanted to build a brand," he says. "There were lots of charities that had been around for a long time. But there was no Nike. There was no Apple. Charities are some of the worst marketers and storytellers."

Harrison invested time and energy in the marketing side of the nonprofit. He lined up donors, even creating a membership society for those who gave substantial long-term commitment—The Well. One of them, PopCap cofounder John Vechey, who has donated $3 million and counting to charity: water, told *Inc.* magazine: "I felt like I spent money to hire smart people, who will do exciting new things and reach way more people."

Nearly 40 minutes into the presentation, the crowd has learned Harrison's story, why he started the company, and how it would be different. They are then told about the incredible fundraising campaigns corporations and individuals have undertaken and the results of their efforts. You can feel the energy of those seated in the room. And then comes the most powerful moment.

Harrison talks about Rachel Beckwith, who for her 9th birthday set the goal of raising $300 for charity: water. She fell short, raising only $220. She hoped to raise more next year, but that chance would never come. Rachel was killed in a car accident soon after her birthday. She may have been gone, but her spirit was still alive, as was her reactivated charity: water campaign. Donations started to come in, first $9 at a time then more and more. A few months after her death, Rachel's charity: water campaign raised $1.2 million. Harrison tells the audience how he asked Rachel's mom to come to Africa to see the results of Rachel's campaign on the one-year anniversary of her death.

He then plays a poignant video of Rachel's mom and grandparents in Ethiopia where they meet the beneficiaries of her campaign. By the time it ends, there isn't a dry eye in the house.

It's hard to imagine any other charity using that combination of storytelling and marketing (with such an investment in high end production value) to make such a powerful pitch to potential donors. Harrison has made this presentation hundreds if not thousands of times. But he still delivers it with the same mixture of passion and empathy.

Since its foundation, charity: water has helped more than 6.1 million people receive clean, safe drinking water by funding over 19,000 water projects in 24 countries.

As if charity: water's work to help end the water crisis wasn't enough, it's also working to end another crisis. Harrison is challenging the Charity Industrial Complex. Until social entrepreneurs and other innovative thought leaders interceded, charities were stuck between a rock and a hard place. The Charity Industrial Complex has one victim: charities. It has held back their growth, dampened their success, and reduced their efficiency. Unable (or unwilling) to break out of the Charity Industrial Complex, charities have been unfairly tarred and feathered by so-called watchdog groups that look for the wrong metrics and a wary public unsure if their donations are well spent.

## THE THREE PILLARS

There are three basic characteristics of the Charity Industrial Complex. First, it holds that charities should be meek in overhead but mighty in intentions. Second, it presupposes that guilt is the most effective tool to build donor support. Third, charities reward the act of giving without tying directly to impact.

It's a common refrain: "How much of my money will go into the field and how much to overhead?" Overhead is the bane of charities' existence. They must keep it as low as possible or face public shaming. Charities have been hampered by their own approach and by societal expectations. Overhead to charities is like a big nose. It gets pointed out over and over again and eventually the person (or in this case, charities themselves) develop a complex about it.

"The things we've been taught to think about giving and about charity and the nonprofit sector are actually undermining the causes we love and our profound yearning to change the world," Dan Pallotta said in his powerful 2013 TED Talk. He was referencing our aversion to overhead.

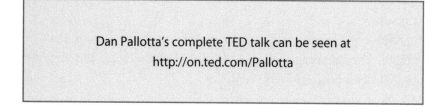

Dan Pallotta's complete TED talk can be seen at
http://on.ted.com/Pallotta

Charities are praised for frugality. They are admired for low overhead and limited marketing. At the same time they are criticized if they spend too many resources on staff or on any item that doesn't deliver resources to the field. With little money for marketing, and no focus on branding, it is little wonder *The New York Times* columnist Nicholas Kristof once commented, "Any brand of toothpaste is peddled with far more sophistication than the life-saving work of aid groups."

So charities can't spend money on building their brand, marketing, advertising, or raising public awareness about their cause. If they did, they would become pariahs. Despite the fact that these tools are considered essential parts of the business toolbox, they are off limits to charities. Why? Isn't it valuable to create brands that can be leveraged for causes important to society? Shouldn't the organizations that are trying to save the world market themselves with the same tenacity as Crest?

Being meek in overhead creates another unintended problem. Charities aren't able to focus on what many see as their biggest shortcoming: transparency. Harrison was well aware of this obstacle when he founded charity: water. By setting up those two separate bank accounts and being transparent, Harrison solved this problem. People always told him that charities were black holes. "The transparency stops the minute the donor gives," Harrison told me when I visited the new charity: water headquarters in Lower Manhattan. "I assume charities are always trying to have an impact, but they did a bad job connecting donors to that impact." With its separate but equal (in importance if not size) bank accounts, charity: water could spend money, energy, and time building a platform to connect donors to their impact. "How simple. How clear. How definitive," he said. "I did that with two bank accounts with $100."

The second tenet of the Charity Industrial Complex is the method by which charities encourage donations. They use guilt. Guilt can come in many forms. You've probably gotten pieces of mail with sad images of people in despair. You may have seen infomercials with slow, dark-sounding music, filled with images of melancholy kids. The charities' message to the donor is twofold. First, they hope to make you feel so bad about the situation that you will donate. Second, they want to play off the Puritan belief that charity is a form of penance. So if this kind of suffering is foreign to you and you are living a comfortable life, you should give something back.

Harrison didn't believe in donations by guilt. He tried it another way. He made it cool. "It should be cool to give. It should be cool to be generous. It should be cool to say yes to helping out," he said. Instead of making people feel guilty, Harrison wanted them to feel excited and hopeful. That meant an entirely new way to brand. Look at the images that charity: water displays on its site or in its marketing materials. They are powerful. They are poignant. They are positive. Its subjects are smiling; they look hopeful for a better future, a future that is delivered to them by the help of donors.

"I think so many charities for years have operated in shame and guilt. Let me make you feel as bad as possible about yourself so you will then reach into your wallet and give. For us it is much more invitational. It is a great opportunity not based in guilt or shame," Harrison told me. "No one is going to wear a T-shirt about an organization that makes you feel lousy about yourself. But we do wear T-shirts from Nike because Nike makes us feel great about ourselves. Nike believes that within us is greatness."

That feeling of hopeful inspiration doesn't extend only to the donor base of charity: water. It extends to the office environs and staff. In 2015, charity: water moved into a new office in Lower Manhattan. It may be the coolest office I've ever seen (and I work in real estate, so I've seen a lot). The office feels more like a tech startup than a nonprofit. There are creative spaces for meetings, whiteboard walls, Millennials buzzing everywhere, oversized displays with inspirational messages (including one huge yellow wall that reads "#nothingiscrazy"). There is a maternity room, a coffee bar, a think tank, and shuffle board and ping-pong tables. There are two water

## CHARITY AS "CARITAS"

Charity is derived from the Latin word *caritas*, which in essence means "love." But the word has nothing to do with the recipients of that love. It has everything to do with its donors. The late Duke University professor Greg Dees noted, "We're rewarding people for demonstrating their love of humankind, but we're not often looking to see whether it has the intended impact." Dees also believed that we honor the wrong metric. We honor how much people give. *Chairman's Circle. Founders Ring. Benefactor. Friend.* Honors go to those who give the largest amount of money. But why not instead honor those that make the biggest impact? Then maybe we would come to know other designations. *Savior. Hero. Champion. Difference-maker.* Doing so would promote what is supposed to be the entire point of charity: change.

St. Thomas Aquinas addresses caritas in his *Summa Theologiae* Part 2, Question 23. Charity, when executed to truly benefit others, is caritas, according to St. Thomas. However, when done for one's own conscience, it is not caritas. It is a self-serving way of flaunting power that has nothing to do with the intended principles of charity.

wells with pumps. There's a state-of-the-art sound room, video-editing room, dashboards that highlight the nonprofit's metrics in real time, and modular desks by Steelcase. Most of the items that make up the 22,000-square-foot space were donated or purchased at heavily discounted prices. Newmark Grubb Knight Frank, the commercial real estate conglomerate, graciously leased the space to charity: water at an enormous discount to its market value.

Harrison's office is modern with large sliding glass doors, modern furniture, and a writable wall. "Working in an organization with your vocation, it doesn't need to be a bummer," Harrison told me. "I don't think you need to walk around with a sad face all day because you are working in conditions of extreme poverty."

The third principle behind the Charity Industrial Complex is that charities need not focus on impact and results but instead on the act of giving.

Instead of adopting a laser focus on giving, Harrison went one step further. He wanted to connect donors to their impact. I've donated to many charities, including charity: water. But no other charity has connected me to my donations like it has. I have GPS coordinates on all the water projects I've funded and can view them on Google Earth. A clean-water rig that I helped fund has its own Twitter account (@ cwyellowthunder) and sends out regular updates on its progress.

Whereas charity: water embraces impact, many older charities have left that in the background. "Because the norms of charity permeate this sector, organizations have only needed to show charitable intent and tell good stories to motivate caritas in board members, donors, and staff, so that they survive and even thrive, regardless of their impact," Greg Dees noted in his remarkable paper "A Tale of Two Cultures: Charity, Problem Solving, and the Future of Social Entrepreneurship."

Since charity: water's emergence, a new generation of charities has followed in its trailblazing path. Together they are remaking how we give, what we give, and why we give. They are working to break the Charity Industrial Complex.

## A CITY UPON A HILL

Why has the Charity Industrial Complex been so hard to eliminate? The hardest habits to break are those that have been with us the longest. The Charity Industrial Complex has been part of America since before its founding. Its arrival even predates the earliest colonists.

In the spring of 1630, a flotilla of 11 ships set sail from the Isle of Wight in England bound for the Massachusetts Bay Colony. Aboard were some 700 Puritans who sought more than just their religious freedom. They also sought fortune. Known for their piety more so than their prosperity, the Puritans were awash with contradictions.

The Puritans wanted to make money. But they also wanted to avoid eternal hell. So they came up with a way to salvation—charity. As Dan Pallotta has commented: "Charity became their answer. It became this economic sanctuary where they could do penance for their profit-making tendencies—at five cents on the dollar. So of course, how could you make money in charity if charity was your penance for making money?"

To remove any doubt, at some point during the journey, John Winthrop delivered his "Model of Christian Charity" sermon. He begins the sermon by stating, "God Almighty, in his most holy and wise providence, hath so disposed of the condition of mankind as in all times some must be rich, some poor, some right and eminent in power and dignity; others mean and in subjection." The colony, he declared, would be a Puritan "city upon a hill." Individuals, not large corporations or associations, Winthrop argued, best facilitated charity work. Winthrop's sermon set the tone for the next 350 years of charity practice in the new world. Charity wasn't designed as salvation for those in need; it was created as salvation for the wealthy who needed saving. Big difference. For those 350 years charity in America has functioned with two hands bound behind its back.

## THE CHARITY CIRCUIT

Charity has been a powerful force in American life. According to the National Philanthropic Trust, in 2014, more than $358 billion was donated to charity. That represented 2.1 percent of our entire GDP. And 98.4 percent of all high-net-worth households give to charity. By 2015, more than 1,521,000 registered charities existed in the United States. It's estimated the charitable donations in the first half of the 21st century may exceed $50 trillion.

Throughout history people have graciously and generously plowed billions of dollars into organizations only to see the underlying issues behind those problems become worse and worse. The money often finds its way not to those in need, but to those in leadership of despotic regimes. And even when it reaches its intended beneficiary, the money often does not deliver the kind of help it intends.

But charity has been good for one group. It has been good for donors.

Charity is altruistic. It feels good to give. At the high end of the giving network, the 1 percenters of giving, charity becomes part of a never-ending circuit of events and benefits intended to help a specific group or cause. Tickets for events can cost between $5,000 and $10,000, and the cost of formal attire can run over $20,000. *New York Magazine* commented: "The charity circuit, once a bastion of breeding and privilege, has transformed itself, in the days since 9/11, into a kind of reality show. Running from September through May (and ending with the Met's Costume Institute Benefit Gala), the parties raise funds but also provide an extended publicity campaign for young women who seek to become famous."

Before social entrepreneurs disrupted charity and broke the Charity Industrial Complex, it had become all about the donor instead of its impact. For too long charity was a self-perpetuating, self-sustaining, and self-aggrandizing affair. Some did it to feel good about themselves and hoped it made a difference. To others it was an accessory item—nothing more than a Birkin bag.

The way traditional charities and nonprofits operate is in desperate need of revision. For many, joining the board of a nonprofit or charity is the start of a "second act." It's a chance to repay society for all the opportunities it has afforded. Those who work at one know the trade-offs all too well: low pay, small overhead, tiny marketing budgets. Money raised belongs in one place—in the hands of those the organization seeks to serve. We are all too familiar with this model. And it's all wrong.

The social entrepreneurs shaped by The Great Convergence have disenthralled themselves from conventional norms. They are posing new questions and getting new results. Why do we herald an entrepreneurial creator of an app that allows users to grow a virtual farm and in turn makes billions of dollars, yet we expect the leader of a nonprofit that develops innovative ways to farm in Nigeria to make no money? Why are nonprofits held to a lower standard than for-profit companies? Shouldn't all companies, regardless of tax status, find ways to succeed financially?

The nonprofit and charity space had been perceived as the backwater of business, the place you went if you couldn't cut it in the for-profit world. Not anymore.

Today, some of the most innovative, thoughtful, and game-changing social entrepreneurs run nonprofits and charities. And yes, they, too, are social entrepreneurs. Prominent investment banker and entrepreneur Atul Tandon recently told *Forbes* magazine: "The nonprofit label in my mind is simply a label that denotes the tax system, the IRS enterprise. In my mind, however, the term 'social enterprise' is defined differently. It's an enterprise that is focused on building the social good, the common good."

Social entrepreneurs are entering the charity and nonprofit sector at just the right moment. They are disrupting traditional approaches and forcing new conversations about what makes the best approach to problem solving. They are exploring new ways to scale, new ways to advertise, and new ways to generate revenue. They are borrowing from the best of the for-profits. And by doing so, they are creating a new foundation for success.

"We need to be open to bigger, bolder reform because the hard truth is Philanthropy 1.0 hasn't worked well enough," former AOL chair Steve Case said back in 2006. "If you'll forgive the computer metaphors, our system needs an upgrade."

One of those upgrades has been the movement toward revenue streams at nonprofits and charities. These hybrid models have enabled them to become less dependent on donor support, more self-reliant, and more scalable. This is all designed to maximize the organization's ability to meet its goal. The hybrid model is a significant departure from the more traditional leveraged nonprofit model, which requires outside philanthropic funding to achieve its goals.

In late 2015, Mark Zuckerberg announced that he and his wife, Dr. Priscilla Chan, plan to give away 99 percent of their Facebook shares to charity over the course of their lifetime. While this historic level of gifting is amazing in its own right, how it was structured is equally unique. Rather than establish a foundation as a nonprofit or hybrid, the Zuckerbergs set it up as an LLC. This allows them the ability to invest in other social ventures, including for-profit ones, without being beholden to IRS requirements that accompany traditional nonprofit vehicles.

Emmett Carson of the Silicon Valley Community Foundation observed that this kind of giving may be a harbinger of things to come. "We are at the cusp of a new renaissance in philanthropy, where younger donors in the tech industry are making commitments at a much younger age and are prepared to make much larger commitments," Carson said. "They are using various hybrid tools to carry out that philanthropy here at home, but also around the world."

## THE FOLLY OF FREE SHIRTS

That gets us back to the assertion that charity simply hasn't worked to end global poverty. Handouts haven't worked to fix the underlying problems that plague the developing world. It's not what people want. It's not what they need. We see this time and time again, and it is a lesson that for some reason remains unlearned.

In fact, you could argue that handouts have made things worse. Florida T-shirt marketing guru Jason Sadler found that out the hard way.

In 2010, Sadler had what he thought was a great idea. He was going to collect 1 million T-shirts and over time deliver them to parts of Africa under the campaign "Share the wealth, share your shirts—we're going to change the world." Sadler was motivated to do good. After all, he had seen countless other governments, companies, and individuals donate far more than T-shirts. What could be the harm?

Sadler's intentions were noble. He had already proven himself to be a savvy marketer; companies paid him to wear T-shirts with their logos on them. To him, this was a way he could give back using his T-shirt acumen as a vehicle. He was just trying to make a difference. And had his campaign launched, a difference he would have made—for the worse. By inundating markets with free T-shirts, the local entrepreneurs who were making T-shirts would get severely impacted. It would have resulted in job loss and decreased economic activity, and it would further the false narrative that free give-outs can solve poverty.

The T-shirt giveaway was particularly upsetting to those in Africa who don't have much need for T-shirts. "Millions of Africans who have no trouble getting shirts, who never asked Sadler for a handout, might object to the idea that giving them more clothes will change the world," journalist Nick Wadhams wrote in *Time* magazine. In the developing world, this is referred to as an example of SWEDOW (Stuff We Don't Want).

Sandler's free T-shirt concept was hardly the first SWEDOW of its kind. Since 1997, the National Football League has worked with various charities to provide a very unique handout. The gear arrives like clockwork. In 2009, it came to El Salvador bearing the Arizona Cardinals logo. In 2010, Indianapolis Colts gear came to Haiti. In 2011, Pittsburgh Steeler merchandise arrived in Zambia, Armenia, Nicaragua, and Romania. The 2009 Cardinals, 2010 Colts, and 2011 Steelers were all losers of the Super Bowl.

The NFL and its partners produce merchandise with the name and logo of the winning and losing teams so the items from the winning team can go on sale right after the Super Bowl. In fact, 30 minutes after the New England Patriots won the 2015 Super Bowl, more than one dozen Sports Authority stores were opened for business, selling the championship paraphernalia. As for the losing team, the Seattle Seahawks, their shirts never saw the light of day, at least not here. Until 1996, the NFL destroyed all products with the losing team's logo on them, under the assumption that they had no value. After all, what good is a Seattle Seahawks back-to-back Super Bowl champion shirt if they lost the darn game?

Nonprofit expert Saundra Schimmelpfennig has spoken out extensively against the practice of donating unwanted shirts into a market that does not need them, where no one actually benefits. And there is real harm. When any market is suddenly hit by an influx of supply, prices go down, making it harder for local merchants to make a living.

Kenyan newspaper columnist Rasna Warah summed it up this way to *Time* magazine: "Africa is the greatest dumping ground on the planet. Everything is dumped here. The sad part is that African governments don't say no—in fact they say, 'Please send us more.' They're abdicating responsibility for their own citizens."

Finally, the NFL did take steps to move the donation program in the right direction. They teamed up with a new distribution vendor who asserted, "We only distribute products where communities indicate that they need it."

For some reason, the "developing world needs T-shirts" riff has been calcified in our minds. They don't need T-shirts. Social entrepreneurs understand this. They know how to bring real change and real improvements to the developing world. You know what will change the developing world? Jobs.

## A GREAT ADVENTURE

Becky Straw believes in the power of a job. It has a ripple effect that's far greater than that one person. "What people want most in this world is the opportunity to thrive. Not with handouts, but by using their own two hands," says the website for The Adventure Project, where Straw is cofounder.

It all started with a question. While working to help repair broken water wells in Haiti, Straw was approached by a man who asked, "Are you hiring?" This question would come up again and again.

"I realized the irony that people are desperate to work and we have nobody who has the skills to fix [water] wells. So that's how it started," Straw told *The Huffington Post.*

Since then, she and cofounder Jody Landers have launched The Adventure Project and funded innovative programs on the ground in the developing world that have the potential to achieve scalable results. The Adventure Project connects with and invests in social entrepreneurs who can earn money for themselves while bettering their community.

In fall 2015, The Adventure Project moved into new offices in Manhattan on West 30th Street. I was one of the first visitors to see the space. Straw has a magnetic presence about her. It's easy to see why she has been praised as a pioneer.

Whenever there is a crisis, people are very generous and rush in to offer all kinds of support, she explained to me. But then, "another emergency strikes and people leave. They always leave," she said. It's up to the locals who remain to rebuild their communities. But it can't be done with handouts; they aren't looking for handouts. They want opportunities. That's what The Adventure Project seeks to deliver.

In the five years since inception, The Adventure Project has created almost 800 jobs that have impacted more than 1 million people—jobs in India, Uganda, Kenya, and Haiti. These jobs have included well mechanics, health-care workers, farmers, and stove masons.

In Uganda they've trained health-care workers who can go village to village delivering aid. They are certified to sell 60 products, one of the most popular being the $10 Maama Kit. In Uganda, Straw explained to me, many hospitals and health-care facilities won't admit a pregnant woman in labor unless she brings her own supplies.

"Women save up for these kits," she said. "This is something we would never think about in the developed world." The kits contain plastic sheets, razor blades, gauze pads, soap, gloves, cord ties, and a child health card. The kits' supplies are sterilized and sealed until needed.

Last year Straw and Landers won a DVF Award, The People's Voice. Founded by Diane von Fürstenberg and the Diller-von Fürstenberg Family Foundation, the awards honor the work of incredible women who transform the lives of others. There was an impressive list of successful women present, including Gabrielle Giffords, Hillary Clinton, Tina Brown, Naomi Campbell, Maggie Gyllenhaal, and Dakota Fanning. In the very middle of these remarkable people sat Becky Straw.

The Adventure Project will do its research carefully but it is not afraid to take risks. These risks involve both internal operations and external partners. Straw strives to achieve a balancing act. She is aware of the results that can be achieved with effective marketing, and that means spending money where it needs to be spent. The Adventure Project won't shy away from a challenge, provided there is the ability to scale and create jobs.

The project believes in the power of social entrepreneurs to lift people out of poverty and solve the underlying causes that keep them there. For its 2015 Labor Day campaign, The Adventure Project held a fundraising challenge that allowed the top donors to design a limited edition T-shirt. All donors who chipped in $100 or more would receive the shirt. Now, there's a shirt that can make a difference, even though the Adventure Project didn't lose a Super Bowl.

Muhammad Yunus took direct aim at charity in his book *Banker to the Poor*. "Charity becomes a way to shrug off our responsibility," he wrote. "Charity is no solution to poverty. Charity allows us to go ahead with our own lives without worrying about those of the poor. It appeases our consciences."

Social entrepreneurship is changing this. In that same 1630 sermon in which he outlined his vision for charity, John Winthrop talked about the future world he envisioned. He hoped his new colony would serve "as a city upon a hill." Achieving that vision has been part of our culture ever since. Our leaders from both political parties have used this phrase to frame their policies. But to fulfill it, to truly become that place, it will take change makers to deliver fundamental impact that is beyond party or ideology. We haven't reached it yet. But maybe, just maybe, we are now, finally, on our way.

# bottom of the pyramid

*Human beings are much bigger
than just making money.*

—MUHAMMAD YUNUS

**W**e've known for many years about the economic potential of those at the lower end of the economic spectrum. The Bottom of the Pyramid (BoP) is now fertile ground as the largest consumer market on earth. Instead of looking at the world's poor as a group to be pitied, social entrepreneurs look at them as market to be coveted. From microlending to scalable businesses, social entrepreneurs have changed the way we see the developing world. As a result, there are newfound opportunities to leave poverty behind while creating profits for social entrepreneurs.

But it wasn't always like that.

It was 1932. Times were terrible. The U.S. gross domestic product fell by 13.4 percent that year. Industrial stocks were down 80 percent since their peak. Forty percent of all banks in the U.S. had already failed. Unemployment soared to over 23 percent of the population.

It had been a year and a half since the first supermarket opened. An ambitious governor who sat at the top of the economic pyramid would soon become the 32nd president of the United States. While his wealth could have easily blinded him to the plight of those at the bottom of the economic pyramid, his life experiences taught him otherwise. Polio deprived him of the use of his legs, but it strengthened his resolve to make a difference in the world.

Franklin D. Roosevelt knew what it was like to be forgotten. His once promising political career—he was the Democrats' nominee for vice president in 1920—was largely an afterthought once he received the polio diagnosis. He turned his attention to stamp collecting and reading. When the time came to return to politics, he had a different outlook. During an April 1932 address titled "The Forgotten Man," he shared his thoughts on capital markets with the nation.

"These unhappy times call for the building of plans that rest upon the forgotten, the unorganized but the indispensable units of economic power," Roosevelt said. "[Plans] that build from the bottom up and not from the top down, that put their faith once more in the forgotten man at the bottom of the economic pyramid."

Thus, the concept of BoP entered our lexicon. In Roosevelt's time the workers at larger companies couldn't afford the goods they were producing. It was assumed they were priced out and were not a part of the economy. Roosevelt did not believe this was true. His focus as president would be to build from the bottom up and to create opportunities for the bottom of the pyramid.

Today we use BoP to reference the four billion people in the developing world who earn less than $1,500 a year. This demographic resides in geographies where stable governments, natural resources, and reliable communications networks are circumspect. The work of social entrepreneurs is largely focused on bringing Capitalism 2.0 to this market.

And it isn't just any market. It's worth an estimated $5 trillion, making it the largest untapped market on earth. The products that social entrepreneurs bring change the lives of these consumers.

We all benefit when more people participate in the economy. C.K. Prahalad wrote about this in *The Fortune at the Bottom of the Pyramid*, when he first brought this global market to the forefront. The book was a game changer. Bill Gates referenced it as "an intriguing blueprint for how to fight poverty with profitability." In the decade since, companies have launched products specifically designed for those earning under $2 per day. It isn't easy. With costs fixed, it comes down to scale. You need many consumers for the investment to yield any sort of return. It has been a winding road, as it always is with emerging markets, but some are making it.

## THE ROAD LESS TRAVELED BECOMES A BEATEN PATH

It was the perfect storm for mass suffering. After achieving independence in 1971, Bangladesh quickly entered a crisis. In January 1972, *Time* magazine reported, "In the aftermath of the Pakistani army's rampage last March, a special team of inspectors from the World Bank observed that some cities looked 'like the morning after a nuclear attack.'" An estimated six million homes were destroyed and almost 1.5 million people were left without sufficient equipment to harvest food and crops.

George Harrison, the former Beatle, released a song about the suffering in which he proclaimed: "Bangladesh, Bangladesh / Where so many people are dying fast / And it sure looks like a mess / I've never seen such distress."

But it was about to get worse. In 1974, famine struck. Heavy flooding from the Brahmaputra River wiped out much of the local food supply. The government was caught unprepared for this calamity. It had only been a few years since they won their independence, and those in power had no experience containing such a crisis. The United States had over 2 million tons of food aid that it refused to deploy until Bangladesh stopped supplying Cuba with jute. By the time Bangladesh acquiesced, it was already too late. Deaths from starvation, disease, and the aftermath of the famine reached 2 million people.

Observing the calamity, Muhammad Yunus, then a young professor of economics at the University of Chittagong, went into the field to study why so many people were suffering from the famine. He traveled east to Jobra, a small rural village. There he met a 21-year-old woman named Sufia Begum who was in desperate need of funds to support herself. She had taken out a loan with a local moneylender. The loan amount was 25 cents. The interest rate was 10 percent per day. The loan also required her to sell her wares back to the moneylender at below market price, leaving her with a tiny return of about 2 cents.

Sufia wasn't alone. Yunus was soon introduced to other women who were in the same predicament. The economist in him identified a poverty trap. The humanitarian in him discovered a way to defeat it. To make their bamboo stools, the women needed $27. That's all. Yunus engaged in an experiment. He lent them the money with an interest rate of about 62 cents per borrower. The women were also allowed to sell their product at the fair market price. To his pleasant surprise, 100 percent of this initial loan was repaid. Yunus was on to something.

Excited, he went to the bank on campus at the University of Chittagong to encourage them to lend to the poor of Jorba. "Absolutely no way," he was told by a bank official. "The bank cannot lend money to the poor people."

If the banks weren't going to lend to the poor, Yunus would launch a new bank that would turn the tables on every established lending rule. Banks want collateral. Yunus's bank would not have any of it. Banks lend to men. He would lend to women. And no lawyers. He wouldn't require attorneys or the notarization of documentation. This bank would focus on the poor.

Today, more than 7 million borrowers rely on Grameen Bank. Of those, 97 percent are women. The average loan balance per borrower is approximately $162. The gross loan portfolio of the bank is in excess of $1.1 billion.

The bank makes loans to artisans and to others looking to rise out of poverty. It has financed thousands of college, graduate, and medical students. Grameen Bank has enriched and changed lives, while moving people out of poverty.

And what of the default rate? Do the poor really pay back loans like borrowers do in the developed world? The answer is no.

In the developed world, default rates vary depending on the type of loan. Student loan default rates hover around 11 percent, mortgage default rates are at 6.5 percent, and credit card defaults are slightly under 3 percent.

At Grameen Bank, in a typical year the default rate is 2 percent. The bank's borrowers outperform the payback rate of almost any other bank in the world. Yunus has proved that being poor is not an impediment to being a good investment. It also demonstrates the financial rewards that can be made by turning the BoP into your customers. Grameen Bank has over $176 million in annual revenue through its microfinance programs.

We tend to think of the poor in the developing world as an economic group without clout. How could they have clout if they earn less than $1,500 a year? It is true, on an individual level they lack leverage. But as a collective they are enormous. How big? There are more than 4 billion potential consumers waiting to be tapped. The question for social ventures is: How?

Until recently most ventures stayed clear of the developing world. It just didn't seem like a good business pursuit. "The dominant assumption is that the poor have no purchasing power and, therefore, do not represent a viable market," wrote C. K. Prahalad. By dispelling the mythology about the poor, Prahalad led a counterintuitive argument that ventures should find ways to engage the poor as consumers.

This is a far more appealing option for those living in the BoP than charity. When you are given something for free, you are to be grateful, even if what you've been given is not what you need. But once you move from being a recipient of charity to a consumer of record you have clout. If the product or service isn't what you want, you don't pay for it. If you don't like it, you can voice your complaint. It's an entirely different paradigm. This paradigm shift works not just at the micro level but at the macro level as well.

## GOING BIG

Unilever, the $60 billion juggernaut of consumer goods, has made big bets on the developing world. With more than 400 brands under its umbrella, it reaches consumers all over the globe. Last year almost 60 percent of Unilever's total sales came from emerging markets. Procter & Gamble also has set its sights on emerging markets.

One Procter & Gamble executive told CNN back in 2013 when its new $170 million facility in South Africa was announced: "We are in Africa because of the size. It's about a billion people; that's the size of China and India, for example, just under, and the population is growing, the economies are getting more and more stable, so huge opportunities here. We have businesses in Nigeria, in Kenya, Uganda, Tanzania—we are going to go to Angola, Ethiopia."

Marketing to this unique demographic requires an entirely new approach to marketing. Traditional thinking—like so much else in Capitalism 2.0—requires a reboot.

During a meeting of the American Marketing Association in 1953, Harvard Business School professor and marketing guru Neil Borden coined a new term: the "marketing mix." It is still used to this day to determine what tactics a company will use to effectively sell its products in the marketplace. His four Ps became the bedrock for the emerging discipline of consumer marketing: Promote, price, product, and place are the four elements that made up Borden's marketing mix.

For the BoP, Prahalad developed a different marketing mix. He takes into account the special circumstances, obstacles, challenges, and opportunities of reaching those in this market. His four A's are: awareness, access, affordable, available.

Underlying his four As is the scale that sellers to the BoP need to achieve. When you are selling product at very low prices, the only way to make a profit is with volume. High market penetration is paramount. In some markets as much as 30 percent penetration is required for profitability. Such large-scale user adoption means consumers are aware your product exists, they have access to it, the price point works within the budget of the local community, and it is easily available for purchase.

In the developing world, where roads, infrastructure, and technology can be limited, there are added challenges to awareness, access, affordability, and availability that don't present themselves in the developed world.

## MAKING IT SCALE

Social entrepreneurs must adapt their skill set to accommodate the special conditions of the BoP. As a result, they focus much more on Prahalad's four A's than Borden's four Ps. Doing so enables them to thrive. That's exactly what John Anner's organization is doing in Vietnam.

A little over a decade ago, East Meets West was a typical nonprofit organization. It had an annual budget of $225,000 with one U.S.-based staffer and the rest in Vietnam, where they did grassroots work to help the poor.

"We do nice things for the poor people of Vietnam" is how the current CEO, John Anner, described the organized prior to its reboot. "There was no effort to scale, no evidence approach, no data analysis, or anything like that at all."

At the time, East Meets West did not need any of those tools. What they were doing "was a viable business proposition," Anner told me. It was also par for the course. This was the way your typical nonprofit would operate.

Times have changed.

Today, reconstituted as Thrive Networks, the organization has provided assistance to more than 3 million people. Thrive disaggregates its work into three areas: health, water, and education.

Thrive Networks has accomplished all this by transforming itself from a traditional nonprofit to a social innovator. What's the difference? It starts with scale.

Traditional nonprofits are like rays of sunlight. It's great to be a flower basking in the sunlight, but for everyone else in the shadows, the nonprofit provides no sustenance. Thrive wanted to increase its shine, which meant more scalable solutions and innovative ideas.

To achieve this, Thrive created a network and asked others in the industry to join. Businesses talk all the time about being lean and mean. As Anner learned, there are real hazards for nonprofits that try a similar feat because of how nonprofit capital markets are structured. A $500,000 annual nonprofit has almost no chance of receiving a million-dollar grant. So smaller nonprofits are constantly chasing smaller grants of $20,000 to $300,000, and that makes growth very difficult.

Anner surveyed the marketplace and did not like what he saw. "All of these little nonprofits competing for funding—it's a stupid model," he said.

For the founders of smaller nonprofits, there is real opportunity cost that comes with chasing low-dollar grants. They aren't spending time in the field or doing the core work of their nonprofit. Instead, they are fundraising, fundraising, fundraising. With that kind of attention to raising money, they might as well serve in Congress.

Nonprofits are not just on the fundraising treadmill; they are in the fundraising Hunger Games. The competition for funds is fierce and there are thousands of potential competitors in the landscape.

Anner had an idea. He wanted to try something different. He asked his colleagues, "Why don't we restructure our entire organization as a platform for scaling impact? Instead of doing it ourselves, let's find other organizations and invite them to join the platform."

Anner turned competition into collaboration. "Putting together all these really talented and smart people who know how to run big projects in the same room has opened up whole new horizons of impact for us that we couldn't do before," he said. "Now all the expertise is in-house."

So when Thrive's health-care team needs to design a training program for nurses in Uganda to help improve newborn care, it turns to training experts on staff. There is no lost time or effort in finding the right group to assist in the project. Added resources allow them to have a fast-moving approach to the work and at the same time the ability to do it at a higher level of scale.

And Thrive doesn't just work with nonprofits. It is agnostic to structure. One of its biggest successes involved a for-profit Vietnamese company that Thrive got off the ground. MTTS (Medical Technology Transfer and Services) launched in 2004 with the goal of providing innovative, cost-effective health-care solutions for newborns that require intensive care.

Anner saw an early prototype for a high-intensity phototherapy device that treats severe jaundice. Phototherapy is a highly effective treatment of jaundice, but for hospitals without this machine, the consequences can be severe. Jaundice in newborns can cause long-term health problems, brain damage, and even death when not properly treated. MTTS wanted to solve this by creating a device that could be effectively deployed in Vietnam. Anner reviewed the early model and knew it would not succeed.

"It was inefficient, it didn't deliver enough clinical benefit, and it was ugly," he said. "Doctors didn't want to use it." Anner leveraged Thrive's fundraising network and put money together to hire Design that Matters, a design firm in Massachusetts. There the device was completely overhauled.

## INTELLIGENT DESIGN

Design that Matters CEO Timothy Prestero leapt at the challenge. For years he had been passionately working to create an impactful product that could reach the market in poor nations. In 2010, he created a neonatal incubator he thought would serve thousands of children. *Time* magazine featured the device in its "50 Best Inventions of 2010" list, but the only child ever helped by the product was the one used in the photo shoot. Eager to use his design skills to make a difference, Prestero dove into redeveloping the product. While it was beautiful his team failed to consider several factors including who would manufacture, distribute, and regulate it.

One treatment option for severe jaundice is a risky blood transfusion, which could lead to serious and potentially fatal complications. But, as Prestero told an audience during TEDxBoston in June 2012: "There's another solution. It's a little complex; it's a little daunting. You gotta shine blue light on the kid." Armed with engineering degrees from MIT and University of California at Davis, he set out to engineer a new solution.

Timothy Prestero's complete talk can be viewed at
https://www.youtube.com/watch?v=WpldYJ3sSlo

At the time, most phototherapy devices in places like Vietnam were donated from hospitals in the developed world. The devices were old, used, and most likely had been phased out in favor of a newer model. Rather than throw them away, they were typically donated. It turns out that throwing the devices away may have been more productive. For hospitals in the developing world, they just don't work. The end user is different. Because of overcrowding, doctors would place multiple babies under the light, which impairs effectiveness. Mothers would add blankets fearing their babies were cold, which reduced the amount of light therapy the babies received. And when a device needed repair, no one had the skills to fix it.

The MTTS product that Thrive Networks first explored could be a viable treatment option if only it had a better design. Prestero and his team got to work. They ensured the device could only be used on one baby at a time. They made it work even if a mother put a blanket on a child. It was designed so intuitively that it was almost impossible to misuse. And it looked cool. This turned out to be a key factor in its success. "It sounds crazy and dumb, but they don't want anything that looks cheap and crummy, so it has to look trustworthy," he said. "Every doctor wants Buck Rogers." Well, they got it.

Soon after the redesign was completed, this new phototherapy device, called the Firefly, began to arrive at hospitals across Vietnam. The Firefly delivers impressive clinical benefit and looks modern and sleek. Doctors embraced it. Patients loved it. The results were immediate.

"The MTTS Firefly is very easy to use and the most effective phototherapy we have," Associate Professor Dr. Hla Myat Nwe of the Yangon Children's Hospital in Myanmar told Thrive Networks. "It has helped us avoid many exchange transfusions—the most severe cases that we couldn't treat before. Now we can!"

Infant mortality has plummeted in hospitals using this and other products created by MTTS, increasing demand for its products and services. All this leads to increased revenue for the company.

Thrive Networks retains a portion of MTTS profits, which it then plows into other ventures or programs. Thrive accounts for 60 percent of all MTTS's sales. Using their ability to raise money through donations and grants, Thrive then puts the Fireflys into hospitals around the world.

This amazing collaboration between the nonprofit and for-profit spheres has bred innovation, scale, social benefit, and a growing business. It further demonstrates that the tax status of a venture has no bearing on its ability to achieve success as a social entrepreneurial endeavor. The model created by Thrive Networks shows the power that can be harnessed when both spheres work together.

In the case of the Firefly collaboration, Prahalad's four A's are all at work. Thrive ensured that the hospitals were made aware of this product through their extensive network of doctors and staff around Vietnam. They were able to make the product accessible to each facility. They made it affordable by donating the Firefly, and then MTTS offered additional services to the hospitals. The Firefly was in production and ready for deployment so MTTS could deliver it when needed.

As for the old thinking that nonprofits weren't innovative or problem solving, that has long been dismissed by those in the know. "If you went to work for a nonprofit, it was because you couldn't cut it in the for-profit world. You were a wooly-headed do-gooder," Anner told me. "But now you are getting really highly talented people coming into the nonprofit sector."

## BE A LIGHT IN THE WORLD

No matter the sector, opportunities are now ripe in the BoP. The only question is who will harvest them. For d.light cofounder Sam Goldman, the light went on in his head, and by the start of the next decade, he intends for it to shine on 100 million people.

Goldman's imagination was ignited by kerosene. In the developing world this combustible hydrocarbon is frequently found in the home for everyday uses, including lighting. "The thing that really sparked me was my next-door neighbor," Goldman said. He had been working in the Peace Corps in Benin, Africa, when he witnessed firsthand the hazards of kerosene. Upon returning to the village one day, he saw a boy covered in leaves and herbs. He had third-degree burns all over his body. In the darkness of the house, he had accidentally knocked over kerosene, it ignited, and the resulting fire left him burned. It could have been worse. The neighbors' house was made of mud, not straw, so the fire did not engulf the home and put the village at risk.

Goldman had been bugged for a while at the heavy amount of kerosene use in the village. He assumed there was a better, safer way for villagers to light their homes. Goldman saw an opportunity for a business that could provide this alternative. "I had been writing companies in the U.S. and Europe that had been producing LED headlamps or other battery-powered LED products to say, 'Hey, there is a massive market here. How can we do business together? I'll be your distributor!'" Not one company bothered to respond. Now Goldman was more than bugged.

He started researching alternative lighting sources. He experimented with an LED and stopped using kerosene altogether. It changed his life in Africa. People in the village asked where they could get the light and how much it cost. Goldman knew this was more than a good idea. This was a business.

Over the years he had witnessed firsthand the huge amount of money thrown into the developing world in the form of aid. Sure, some of it was helpful. But it was hardly efficient, and any change it brought was slow moving. What brought powerful and lasting change was capitalism. "When you become much more free market and capitalistic, things change so fast," he told me. "Everything to me was, it's going to happen one way or another, and we can do it properly so that it's going to have the most benefit for the poor and vulnerable, or it won't." Goldman saw it for himself. Nothing can bring about change—positive, meaningful change—like Capitalism 2.0.

Goldman returned to the U.S. and enrolled in Stanford's Design for Extreme Affordability course. There he met Ned Tozun, and together they committed themselves to making a solar product that would provide a safe, clean, and affordable solution to those living in the BoP with their new venture, d.light.

This was an enormous undertaking. First, the product didn't exist. d.light would need to create an affordable device that consumers would spend their hard-earned money on. Second, the category didn't exist. There was no such thing as a safe lighting alternative market. Third, the brand didn't exist. But by overdelivering on a great product, d.light felt it could overcome those hurdles. Goldman observed, "what we have done that nobody else cracked was how do you make a sub-$10 product that has unbelievable quality and destroys the current alternative, and how do you do all the things you need to do to get them to people to touch, feel, and use the product?"

Two billion people rely on kerosene as a light source. Kerosene isn't cheap and it isn't even a great light source. Where some might see an intractable problem, d.light saw a market. In a marvelous feat of engineering, d.light brought to market in 2008 solar lanterns that were durable, powerful, and beautifully designed. The market reaction was powerful.

The demand for d.light's array of solar products has been insatiable. They have more than 51 million customers in more than 60 countries. Thirteen million school-aged children now have solar-powered lighting for reading. The net savings to their customers, by using d.light products over traditional ones, is more than $1.8 billion. Replacing kerosene with solar has prevented the release of more than 4 million tons of carbon monoxide into the atmosphere.

There is a simple element to d.light's product that helped them grow so quickly. They were selling light. "The first day you take it home you realize the benefits, and they are obvious," Goldman said. The life improvement is abundantly clear. It isn't like changing a water system and then telling someone they won't get sick later or bringing a new curriculum into a school so the child will learn a vocation. This product provides instant gratification and validation. This advantage helped the company grow, as did its other, equally important advantage: timing.

Everything came together at precisely the right moment for d.light. LED prices dropped. Solar panel prices dropped. Battery prices dropped. "We are in the perfect market. We had this technology convergence happen for totally separate reasons, exactly at the time that the social enterprise space exploded," Goldman said.

Most of d.light's customers aren't used to being consumers. Historically they have not consumed a lot. Many grow their own food and haven't entered the global economy. But that is starting to change. Not only are they now becoming consumers, but they are also becoming smart consumers with the ability to purchase products that are safe and beneficial for their lives.

While attending the Global Entrepreneurship Summit in Kenya during summer 2015, President Obama declared, "Africa is on the move." After delivering his remarks he met with several social entrepreneurs, including Goldman, who gave him a demonstration of the d.light solar lamps.

"With you right here in Kenya, we are launching a game changer," Goldman said to the president when he approached the d.light demonstration booth outside the summit. He held up a rugged square-shaped product and gave it to President Obama. "It's called the A-1. It's small; it's tough. You can drive a car over it; you can throw it off the White House roof."

"Oh, I'm not going to do that," quipped the president, who marveled at the size and strength of the device. "And this will last me all through the night?" he asked Goldman, who assured him it would.

d.light is already more than halfway to its 2020 goal of transforming 100 million lives in the developing world. Transformative change often involves introducing a new product or service to the developing world. Other times it entails bringing products to the developed world at the hands of highly skilled workers in the developing world. By serving as a global matchmaker of social change and innovation, one nonprofit is taking artisan empowerment to a whole new level.

## BUILD A NEST

It could have been a giant cinderblock. It certainly would have cost less and it would have served the same general purpose. Soon to rise in Varanasi, India, is a breathtaking structure to house silk artisans. Designed by celebrity architect David Adjaye, the facility will reflect Buddhist-Moghul-Hindu architecture and the values of the area. A 500-year tradition in this region of the world, handmade silk crafting has come under tremendous pressure from machines that can produce products faster, although at a lower level of quality. As an industry it faces extinction in as little as a decade. Some have argued that the tide of history cannot be turned. Silk artisans, they contend, should be retrained and re-enter the workforce in a different capacity. Rebecca van Bergen will have none of that.

"These people are not laborers; this is an incredibly amazing and intricate craft. They are artists. They deserve a beautiful space to work," van Bergen told me. "And luxury fashion houses should see this as a luxury craft. So how do we shine a spotlight on this craft? A cinderblock building isn't going to do it."

Empowering artisans and connecting them to the global marketplace has been van Bergen's passion since she started Nest almost a decade ago. It's been a long journey. Her advocacy, action, and audacity on behalf of the artisans of the developing world started back in a St. Louis coffee shop.

In 2006, van Bergen had just obtained her master's degree in social work. Like many in her generation, she was a well-educated achiever. But what to do with her degree? She was frustrated. She had so many different interests and passions, it seemed like no profession out there could combine her talents.

Adding to her frustration, she had recently been told not to even bother applying for a business loan. She wanted to open a store and sell merchandise created by foreign artisans. The bank felt that she was a bad bet. She had no business experience and no collateral. Despite her noble effort, the loan was a nonstarter.

"I ended up listing all the things I liked on a sheet of paper, trying to come up with something that fulfilled many of my interests: working with women and children, social activism, international travel, fashion, design, art, and the green movement," she later said. A job that combined all those didn't exist, so van Bergen decided to create it. And in doing so, she created a company that is helping to change the world. She started to build Nest, and she has never looked back.

Nest helps artisanal businesses connect to the global market. They perform an assessment and, depending on what is needed, can do everything from invest in infrastructure upgrades to provide skill development and business training. They create customized programs and devise a plan for scalable business development. And they connect artisans to retailers who are seeking high-quality handmade products.

For the retailers, Nest provides assurance that the artisans meet ethical compliance and professional standards of excellence. This is a major issue for retailers who are interested in working with those in the developing world. Brands need to be careful whom they employ. "There are quality control issues, there are communication issues, there are timing issues," van Bergen told me. Nest addresses all these issues without resorting to an intermediary as the solution. This concept is very important to van Bergen. She wants to elevate the artisans so they can enter the marketplace themselves instead of being beholden to a middleman to get them there. This model is remarkably empowering and sustaining for the artisans.

Interestingly enough, Nest did not start out with this model. At first Nest issued microloans to artisans, who used the proceeds to purchase tools and materials for their products. Nest then sold the products and repaid the loan with the proceeds. Five years ago the company made a strategic shift. "We were fostering a model of dependency," van Bergen said. "The artisans were relying on a nonprofit intermediary to get to market. From my perspective there is an ethical dilemma. Artisans weren't getting to market alone." Even though this model had become increasingly popular with other ventures getting into the space, van Bergen was set on changing course. So Nest stepped out of the supply chain and became a third-party intermediary. As a result, Nest now puts the artisans in the global marketplace.

Nest works with thousands of artisans around the world. They are in India, Indonesia, Kenya, Mexico, and Swaziland. A Nest artisan earns on average 120 percent more than the local minimum wage. They are leaving behind poverty and oppression and becoming businesspeople, becoming part of the global economy. Eighty-nine percent of Nest artisans are women, who tend to reinvest earned income in food, education, and the community. A ripple effect takes hold. Nest calculates that for every one of its artisans, the ripple effect impacts more than 17 people. Before this decade is out, Nest hopes to bring sustainable change to more than 2 million people.

The remarkable work of Nest, d.light, the Grameen Bank, and thousands of other social entrepreneurial ventures has altered the course of millions of lives. People can only grow, and communities can only succeed, when their needs are met. Writing about this in 1943, psychologist Abraham Maslow presented "A Theory of Human Motivation" as a paper in *Psychological Review*®. He contended that there are five basic human needs which are best expressed on a pyramid, starting from the bottom and rising to the top: physiological, safety, love/belonging, esteem, and self-actualization.

Physiological needs such as air, water, and food are the fundamental requirements for our survival. Maslow viewed these needs as primary. Once they were attended to, needs higher on the pyramid could be addressed. Social entrepreneurs begin at the bottom with this most elemental of needs. And they don't stop there. They work to provide people with tools and a framework to achieve the other levels in Maslow's hierarchy of needs.

Those at the Bottom of the Pyramid are no longer trapped in hopelessness. They are on the move. Once their basic needs are addressed, they can rise on Maslow's hierarchy. At its peak is self-actualization. This is when a person reaches his or her potential. Imagine what is possible once millions of people at the BoP reach this milestone. They won't be in the BoP much longer. That will change everything.

# the kickstarters

*Wars of nations are fought to change maps.*
*But wars of poverty are fought*
*to map change.*

—MUHAMMAD ALI

He started as a bobbin boy. It was an inglorious start to a career. The work was dangerous, even deadly. In the mid-1800s, to keep textile mill production at the fastest possible rate, women at the looms would call for a boy to collect bobbins spun of wool or cotton. This bobbin boy earned $1.20 per week. The days began early, usually at 5:30 A.M. and did not end until 7:30 P.M. He toiled in terrible conditions for six days a week at the age of 13. And yet, the result gave him great pleasure. Years later, in his autobiography, he would write:

"The hours hung heavily upon me and in the work itself I took no pleasure; but the cloud had a silver lining, as it gave me the feeling that I was doing something for my world—our family. I have made millions since, but none of those millions gave me such happiness as my first week's earnings."

During his youth, Andrew Carnegie spent what little free time he had at the library of Colonel James Anderson. Anderson opened up his 400-volume library to "working boys." Carnegie never forgot the importance of books in his life. It was an experience he wished to give to others. And did he ever accomplish that. More than 2,800 libraries around the world were funded by Carnegie.

In fact, Carnegie became a one-man Kickstarter. He supported the work of universities, libraries, hospitals, meeting halls, recreational facilities, and other public benefits. He launched the Carnegie Corporation of New York to "promote the advancement and diffusion of knowledge and understanding." He created a council on ethics and international affairs, an endowment for international peace, and almost a dozen other trusts and funds all with the intention of helping society at large.

By the time he sold Carnegie Steel to J.P. Morgan for $480 million, Andrew Carnegie was done making money. At the age of 65, he turned to his real passion: giving it away. He hoped to die penniless and nearly achieved that goal.

"The man who dies rich," he would write in *The Gospel of Wealth*, "dies disgraced."

Carnegie's Kickstarter philanthropy was extraordinary. He became the standard-bearer for how those in the 1 percent should use their abundant resources and created a model that would be followed by other highly successful Americans. Carnegie lived in the Gilded Age, when staggering wealth for some coincided with staggering poverty for others.

## CARNEGIE REVISITED

Today we live in a global gilded age. According to Oxfam International, the richest 85 people in the world possess a combined wealth equal to the poorest 3.5 billion. The Charity Industrial Complex has churned out billions of dollars, over 350 billion a year. It's all been very noble. But as we learned in Chapter 3, it hasn't done nearly enough in the area of problem solving.

In an op-ed in *The New York Times*, Warren Buffett's son, Peter Buffett, stated: "As more lives and communities are destroyed by the system that creates vast amounts of wealth for the few, the more heroic it sounds to 'give back.' It's what I would call 'conscience laundering'—feeling better about extreme wealth by sprinkling a little around as an act of charity."

Former secretary of labor Robert Reich shares this sentiment. He told *The New Yorker*, "It's certainly admirable that wealthy individuals are willing to give away large chunks of their wealth, but as in the late nineteenth century, when Carnegie, Rockefeller, and others did so, these philanthropic actions are small potatoes relative to the large and growing problems faced by the poor and lower middle class."

But what if there was more to it than giving away "large chunks of their wealth," as Reich suggests? What if the 1 percent were not just writing checks? What if they were investing, consulting, collaborating, and working directly with entrepreneurs around the world to solve problems? What if they became stakeholders and not just check writers? This is an advancement from the age of Carnegie. He agreed that much of charity was not spent well and that results counted. Carnegie wrote that philanthropists "assist, but rarely or never do all." Herein lies the advancement of today's Kickstarters. They may not do all, but they certainly do more than just assist.

Today there is a new group of philanthropists who are redefining what it means to give. In fact, they aren't really "giving." Instead, they are Kickstarters of social enterprise. Just like with the crowdfunding platform, those putting money in expect something in return. The Kickstarters of social enterprise do more than just write a check. Using lessons they've learned from Capitalism 1.0, they can redirect their funds in Capitalism 2.0 and use their Kickstarter as a force for global good.

Unlike past generations that focused on giving, the Kickstarters focus on results. The donor-receiver relationship does not end with the writing and receiving of a check. That's just where the kickstart begins. "I believe philanthropy has fundamentally changed in the last decade from generating headlines about a philanthropist's generosity to an explicit focus on results," said Mark Kramer, cofounder and managing director of the mission-driven consulting firm FSG. "Sophisticated donors today ask not 'How much money was given?' but 'What did the money accomplish?'"

More than check writing, Kickstarters provide social entrepreneurs with all the tools necessary for success. They are diverse organizations that engage in grant making, equity investing, forum organizing, and community connecting. They kickstart, incubate, and mentor the growing social enterprise community.

## OPENING THE GATES

In the 2014 Gates Annual Letter, Bill Gates boldly predicted: "I am optimistic enough about this that I am willing to make a prediction. By 2035, there will be almost no poor countries left in the world. . . . Countries will learn from their most productive neighbors and benefit from innovations like new vaccines, better seeds, and the digital revolution. Their labor forces, buoyed by expanded education, will attract new investments."

Who would have predicted back in 1997—before The Great Convergence—that Bill Gates would be a leader in the fight against global poverty? Needless to say, he has come a long way.

In 1997, above a pizza shop in Redmond, Washington, a new foundation opened for business. Well, if you could call it that. Having made his fortune many times over, Gates took his first baby steps in social enterprise. At first it lacked direction and an identity. A few years later, Gates himself remained ambivalent about the very notion of philanthropy, feeling that it conflicted with his identity as a capitalist. He told Bill Moyers: "I mean, is it going to erode your ability, you know, to make money? Are you going to somehow get confused about what you're trying to do?"

Back in 1997, Gates carried in his briefcase a letter that pained him. A child needed money for a kidney transplant and the family could not afford the $20,000 expense. "Bill agonized over it," Melinda Gates shared at a digital industry conference. "Do you spend $20,000 on a single transplant or buy vaccines for many children in Africa?"

In many ways this has been Gates's mantra: How do you help the most people possible with available resources?

Today, armed with an endowment of more than $42 billion, the Gates Foundation is the most powerful social entrepreneurial and philanthropic force ever unleashed in human history. Over 70 percent of the nations on earth have GDPs less than $42 billion. The Gates Foundation has the kind of power once reserved for governments.

Its projects range from improving health care and education to ending poverty. The foundation doesn't just make grants, either. In 2015, it took a $52 million equity stake in a vaccine manufacturer. But more important is the overall approach the foundation takes to problem solving. It looks at market-based solutions, it looks for enterprising ideas, and it looks at the financial benefits of positive outcomes. It is no surprise *60 Minutes* called him "Bill Gates 2.0." Just like with Capitalism 2.0, Bill and Melinda Gates are applying all they have learned at Microsoft to tackle the world's toughest problems.

Melinda told a reporter back in the foundation's earlier days: "One thing to understand about the foundation is that it's a lot like Microsoft in the sense that we do expect results. We are going to measure things as we go along. We are going to make changes. Sometimes you get other people who come in and do small pieces of this and then their money's spent and they go away. They don't stop to say: What did we learn here and how do we change or how do we replicate that in a new way somewhere else?" This is exactly what differentiates the Gateses' breed of philanthropist from past generations. It's still nice to write a check, but Kickstarters don't stop there.

## IT'S LIKE GETTING INTO HARVARD, ONLY TOUGHER

It's the Harvard of the Kickstarters. Each year more than 3,000 people apply for 40 open slots. Despite the 1.3 percent admission rate, applicants spend hours diligently working on their applications, which are due every November. Fifty percent of the application is based on the venture. The other half is based on the applicant itself.

Once submitted, the application will be reviewed three times by three different teams. From there the list is whittled down to 500–600 people. External evaluators are brought in and the applications are read over again and again. A group of 80 finalists are then invited in for formal interviews, and in June the 40 fellows are announced. Those 40 people are now members of an exclusive club. They are "Echoing Green Fellows."

Some applications are for ventures that are nothing more than paper concepts. Others have piloted their ideas. "We're super early stage," Erica Lock, the dynamic director of fellowship programs for Echoing Green, told me when we sat down to talk in their Manhattan office. Since 1987, Echoing Green has been trailblazing a path for social entrepreneurs. To date, this nonprofit has injected over $40 million into both nonprofit and for-profit ventures. Nearly 700 social entrepreneurs working in more than 60 countries have been kickstarted by Echoing Green. Notable ventures have come out of the fellowship, including Teach for America, Citizen Schools, One Acre Fund, SKS Microfinance, City Year, and College Summit.

Operating with the same approach as a venture capital firm, Echoing Green is investing as much in the person as in the venture. "We invest in the jockey," Lock told me. They aren't just looking for American Pharaoh; they are looking for Victor Espinoza.

Concurring with this sentiment, Echoing Green CEO Cheryl Dorsey recently told an interviewer: "Echoing Green is all about talent. Our capital goes where the talent is, whereas a lot of investment dollars follow business plans or scale propositions. It is our belief that when we invest in next generation leaders, we are really making a bet on finding and supporting transformative and disruptive leaders who will fundamentally change the way we address and solve social issues."

The Echoing Green Fellowship lasts two years, but in many ways it doesn't end. "Once a fellow, always a fellow," Lock told me. Instead of calling former fellows alumni, Echoing Green prefers to keep the fellow moniker to establish a community and continuum.

Once aboard, a newly installed fellow works with a portfolio manager to create an individualized plan and establish goals. Fellows get help with fundraising, business building, operations planning, theory of change, and M&E (monitor and evaluation), and are reminded to stay passionate about their work.

Fellows receive $80,000 (or $90,000 if in a partnership) and $4,000 of health insurance reimbursements, which, it should be noted, goes a very long way in the developing world. They also tap into the vast ecosystem of fellows, advocates, practitioners, professionals, and supporters. Several times a year hundreds of fellows convene at global gatherings. "The philosophy here is that within the supporting [group of] social entrepreneurs, the whole is greater than the sum of its parts," says Lock.

It shouldn't be surprising that Echoing Green is so results-driven. It was founded by General Atlantic, a leading global growth private equity firm. So much of what drove General Atlantic to success has also powered Echoing Green. Both entities have long-term strategies and believe in the virtue of patience.

## THE LEGENDARY BILL DRAYTON

There's a current debate about who should go on the $10 bill. Gender preferences notwithstanding, my vote goes to Bill Drayton. Since 1980, Drayton has been the leader of Ashoka, the granddaddy of the

Kickstarters. His involvement in social entrepreneurship goes back to before the term was popularized. In fact, he coined the term. He may not be a household name, but within the nonprofit community he is a legend.

Since 1981, when the Ashoka Fellows program launched, more than 3,000 social entrepreneurs have received mentoring, training, funding, and access to the ever-growing network of Ashoka fellows. Drayton told one interviewer, "Because they are entrepreneurs, they operate at a level of changing the patterns of society. When new areas of needed social change become ripe, these extraordinary social entrepreneurs appear all over the world." Ashoka fellows are now in 63 countries, where their impacts are profound.

The organization has concentrated on eight areas for social change investment: climate change, energy and environment, transforming modern governance, empowering youth to be change makers, cultural and religious tolerance, innovative social financial solutions, women's livelihood development, bringing disability into the mainstream, news, and knowledge.

Ashoka Fellows candidates undergo a rigorous screening process before they are selected. They are evaluated against five criteria. First, the idea must be a "knockout." Fellowships are offered only to those who have truly new ideas that will bring about change. Second, Ashoka is looking for creativity. The question they are likely to pose is: Does this individual have a vision of how he or she can meet some human need better than it has been met before? Third is the entrepreneurial quality. The candidate needs to have a fire-in-the-belly desire to be engrossed in this venture for the next decade and beyond. Fourth is the social impact of the idea. Ashoka wants ideas that scale up to be transformative. As a result, they would not consider a new health facility or school unless it had bigger aims to make broad change. Lastly, Ashoka probes the ethical fiber of each candidate. Only those they trust beyond question will gain entry into this incredible community.

Initially its work focused on the nonprofit sector, but in recent years Ashoka has broadened its horizons to include for-profit ventures as well.

Over the years, Ashoka and Drayton have received many accolades. They are all earned. *U.S. News & World Report* named him one of America's 25 Best Leaders. Drayton has received the prestigious MacArthur Fellow Award—the so-called "Genius Grant." He's been praised by *Fast Company*, and spoken at the World Economic Forum. So while there is no movement to add Drayton to the $10 bill, he is very content to continue his game-changing work and spread the Gospel of Ashoka. "Anyone can do this," he said. "However, you have to give yourself permission to see a problem and then to give yourself further permission and the time needed to find a solution."

## DOTCOM KICKSTARTERS

Then there are dotcom Kickstarters. Out of the Making Money Now generation came a group that wanted much more. They didn't want more wealth. They had more than they could ever spend. They didn't want more power. They had all they ever needed to accrue. They wanted to make a difference. So after making their billions (and most did before turning 40 years old), they each set out to work harder than ever before. Starting eBay and America Online changed commerce and connectivity. Now they sought to become change makers themselves by kickstarting a new generation of social entrepreneurs. It would have been easy for them to retire and live a rich life. It turns out they do live richly, but it has nothing to do with their wealth. For Jeff Skoll, Pierre Omidyar, and Steve Case it meant deploying their wealth to kickstart the energy, passion, and impact of social entrepreneurs.

Jeff Skoll knows how to tell a story. He grew up in a middle class Jewish family in Canada. In college he pumped gas to earn money. After graduate school and a few stints here and there he met Pierre Omidyar, who had an idea for an online auction business. Skoll didn't think much of it. But Omidyar continued to talk with Skoll about it, and he eventually joined eBay as its first president. Less than three years later Skoll would be a billionaire several times over. Armed with those resources, he set about to achieve his vision: to live in a sustainable world of peace and prosperity.

To achieve that vision, Skoll has unleashed a triple threat of change: the Skoll Foundation, Participant Media, and the Skoll Global Threats Fund.

Since its launch in 1999, the Skoll Foundation has pursued large-scale change through making strategic investments and bringing together leading social entrepreneurs of the world. The foundation has invested an astounding $500 million into more than 100 different ventures on five continents. From clean-water projects in India to health care in Gambia and antiretroviral drugs in Haiti, Skoll has supported and invested in a large portfolio of social entrepreneurs.

The Skoll Foundation accepts nominations from its network of partners but doesn't accept unsolicited nominations for its annual Skoll Awards. It seeks out disruptors who have ideas that can scale, who can collaborate within their ecosystem, and whose social mission is aligned with their vision. Investments are significant, with recipients receiving $1.25 million in funding, support growing their enterprise for three years, and membership to the global community of past and present Skoll Award recipients.

When describing the approach of the foundation, its president and CEO, Sally Osberg, told a reporter: "I said from the beginning, this foundation needed to think and behave more like a social entrepreneur than like a grant-making organization. . . . We leverage our assets to their highest and best use. We're resourceful. We never characterize this foundation in terms of its power or money. We're about the change we're trying to drive and about the difference that's made." Clearly the Skoll Foundation has eschewed past approaches to grant making, which tended to be palliative. Instead its focus is on wholesale change that reshapes the social fabric of society.

To combat threats that could endanger world stability, Skoll launched the Skoll Global Threat Fund to tackle climate change, water scarcity, pandemics, nuclear proliferation, and Middle East conflict.

Relationships with film and TV have helped Jeff Skoll further his far-reaching agenda while highlighting the successes of annual Skoll Award winners. There have been mini-documentaries, specials on PBS, and features at Sundance.

Skoll extended his storytelling ability from the social (entrepreneurial) scene to the silver screen. In 2004, he launched Participant Media and produced such films as *Syriana*; *Good Night, and Good Luck*; *An Inconvenient Truth*; *Fast Food Nation*; *Charlie Wilson's War*; *Darfur Now*; and others. The films have been a tremendous success. They have not only made money, but also created conversations that relate to Skoll's vision on climate change, public health, and foreign policy.

And there is the Skoll Centre for Social Entrepreneurship.

Between the River Thames and Castle Mill Stream in Oxford, England, sits the Saïd Business School. Saïd is a newcomer in the sprawling institution that is Oxford, having been founded in the mid-1990s. Then again everything is relatively new to a university that can trace its roots back to 1096. Since November 2003, it has been home to the Skoll Centre for Social Entrepreneurship. The Skoll Foundation endowed the program with a £4.4 million donation (over $6M in USD). Connecting the worlds of academia and social entrepreneurs with the universe of social entrepreneurs, the Skoll Centre has become a dynamic hub of innovation and energy for the field. Every spring the Centre plays host to the Skoll World Forum, which has become the TED of social entrepreneurship.

Pierre Omidyar learned many business lessons when he built eBay into an e-commerce powerhouse. He saw the opportunities it created for people to start their own business. He saw what happens when people connect, when they have equal access to information, and when market forces are unleashed. Taking those lessons to his own foundation, the Omidyar Network, Omidyar is once again rewriting all the rules. He refers to the foundation as a "philanthropic investment" firm.

"We need to change the way people think about business—to see that it is not inherently evil but inherently good," he told Matthew Bishop and Michael Green in their book *Philanthrocapitalism*. "My sense is that the social sector has acknowledged that, in the end, having a social impact is not the exclusive preserve of nonprofits. Whether you are nonprofit or for-profit, you need to be scalable, need to be sustainable, need to focus on customers and outcomes. No one in the nonprofit sector disagrees."

To make that shift, Omidyar seeks market-based approaches to problem solving that have the ability to scale up. He sees progress and potential to be made by both the for-profit and nonprofit sectors. To that end, investments in for-profit ventures are made through an LLC, and grants to nonprofits are made via a 501(c)(3).

The Omidyar Network focuses on five sectors: consumer internet and mobile, education, financial inclusion, governance and citizen engagement, and property rights.

It's a full portfolio of engagement. Omidyar has committed $810 million since the foundation's 2004 inception. True to its mission of sourcing for solutions no matter where they come from, 44 percent of capital has been invested in for-profit ventures, while 56 percent has gone to nonprofits. "Regardless of the sector, we invest in organizations that have the potential to embody innovation, scale, and sustainability or help bring them about within their industry," the Omidyar Network website says.

## ON THE CASE

"Philanthropy 1.0 hasn't worked well enough; our system needs an upgrade!" Steve Case declared some years back. Case has been a disruptor his entire career. Best known for cofounding America Online, now he and his wife, Jean Case, are changing the world through the Case Foundation.

If Philanthropy 1.0—writing checks and hoping for the best—hasn't succeeded, the Case Foundation is working to ensure its next incarnation is a blazing success. The foundation exists at the intersection of three pillars: igniting civic engagement, unleashing entrepreneurship, and revolutionizing philanthropy. Led by the remarkable Jean Case, the Case Foundation has become an active Kickstarter in social entrepreneurship.

The foundation believes in smart risk-taking. Guided by its five core values—be entrepreneurial, collaborate and learn, experiment early and often, work smart, have fun, be humble—the Case Foundation is in a constant search for new and innovative ways to solve problems.

That means taking risks. The Case Foundation embraces experimentation as a pathway to finding new solutions. Many philanthropies shy away from approaches that are not well-established. But not the Case Foundation. They are fearless when it comes to sourcing and developing new ideas. "We will be a catalyst; we will accept the role of going out early, trying new things and experimenting, and publishing our findings in anything new that we try," Jean Case told me. "We'll take the arrows in the back to try to help figure out what are some new things others can come along and adopt."

As an example, she points to the Case Foundation's early work with contests and grant challenges. The Case Foundation sponsored a summit on innovation at the White House. Thirty-five federal agencies were trained on how to use contests and challenges to drive innovation. Today, Challenge.gov, under the slogan "Government Challenges, Your Solutions," serves as a platform for these challenges. Since its 2010 launch, there have been more than 450 competitions involving more than 200,000 participants that resulted in over $150 million in awarded prizes.

The foundation is bullish on impact investing. The Cases have been impact investors for a number of years. But what Jean finds so promising are the new players who have emerged. "In the past year we've seen unbelievable acceleration and momentum into the sector," she told an interviewer. "We've seen big finance move into the space with some recent announcements. In June we issued a policy report. I sat on an advisory board for the G8 on impact investing, and when we released the report at the White House, we announced $2 billion in new impact investment commitments."

Jean Case is quick to note that investors who once shied away from impact investing are now embracing it. Several years ago Silicon Valley pioneer Marc Andreessen said he would "run screaming from a B Corp." While speaking as a panelist at a conference, he made his feelings on B Corps pretty clear: "The split model makes me nervous, and I don't think we would ever touch that. It's like a houseboat. It's not a great house and not a great boat." Fast-forward a few years. Andreessen's investment firm was part of a $33 million Series A raise for Alt School, a B Corp that is looking to reimagine education through its micro-school and personalized learning program.

"I think this is the tip of the iceberg," Jean Case told *Inc.* "We know there are many organizations poised to make more and bigger commitments, but didn't feel like the timing was right today to come forward. I love that, because it gives us another bite at the apple, if you will."

The Case Foundation recently teamed up with *Forbes*, the Schusterman Family Foundation, the Pratt Foundation, the Keywell Foundation and billionaire entrepreneur Robert Duggan to sponsor the $1 million Forbes Under 30 Change the World Competition.

More than 2,500 applicants entered the competition. From this remarkable group, six finalists were selected. In October 2015 on a stage in Philadelphia, Kiah Williams found herself holding an oversized $500,000 check after being announced as the winner. Williams and her cofounders, Adam Kircher and George Wang, started SIRUM (Supporting Initiatives to Redistribute Unused Medicines) as an online platform to deliver life-saving medicines to those who can't afford them. By sourcing unopened, expired medications and then matching those medicines with people who need them, they have reduced the destruction of safe pills and instead redirected them to people in need. Fifty million Americans can't obtain needed medications each year because of cost. At the same time, $5 billion worth of medications are destroyed or thrown out each year when they are no longer needed. Here is a classic market failure that a dynamic social enterprise is correcting.

The breadth and depth of the Case Foundation's work in social entrepreneurship is impressive. They've announced a partnership with B Lab to create a new initiative called Measure What Matters. They've joined with ImpactAlpha and Entrepreneur.com for a new topic hub on impact investing called Profiles of Impact. They've created a guide to impact investing that helps high net worth individuals and organizations navigate this new terrain. The foundation has provided academic grants and promoted the research being done in some of the finest social entrepreneurial centers around the country.

# THE GLOBALISTS

You don't need to be Carnegie to be a Kickstarter. World leaders and global influencers are now playing an important role in kickstarting change. Two prominent players include Dr. Klaus Schwab and former president Bill Clinton.

In 1971, Dr. Schwab founded the World Economic Forum (WEF) as a nonprofit foundation aimed at connecting business, political, and thought leaders from around the world. Since its humble beginnings, the WEF's annual Davos conference has sprouted into a jet-setting affair featuring elites from all corners of the globe. Presidents and heads of state rub shoulders with international businessmen, celebrities, and media magnates.

Thanks to the international media crush that arrives each year (500 press credentials are typically issued for an event attended by 2,200), along with social media, what happens in Davos doesn't stay there. New ideas get promoted at Davos. With the world's elite gathered in one place, the conference can be a springboard for innovations in problem solving. Understanding the power of the Davos platform, its founder decided to integrate social entrepreneurship into the forum. It turned out to be a perfect marriage.

In 1998, with an endowment from Dr. Schwab and his wife, Hilde, the Schwab Foundation for Social Entrepreneurship has served as a vehicle to advance social entrepreneurs. Each year 20 to 25 social entrepreneurs are selected as part of the foundation's Social Entrepreneur of the Year competition. To date, more than 260 people have received the award and joined this community.

While the Schwab Foundation is a separate entity, it works closely with the WEF. Davos may be the toughest ticket in the world to secure, but not for the social entrepreneurs of the Schwab Foundation. They have the opportunity to attend regional WEF events and of course the annual one held in Davos. This puts social entrepreneurship front and center before global elites.

"Social entrepreneurs are the driving force behind innovations that improve the quality of life of individuals around the world, and they represent an integral and dynamic community of the World Economic

Forum," Hilde Schwab said upon announcing a recent crop of new Social Entrepreneurs of the Year.

Clearly the WEF recognizes the role of the Business of Good in improving the global economy. As corporations now see climate change and global poverty as threats to their long-term stability and growth, they are also looking for solutions. These solutions not only arrest potential losses, they fuel new sources of revenue. "We are seeing greater appetite among other stakeholder groups of the forum to learn from social innovation models and collaborate with social entrepreneurs in innovative ways," David Aikman of the Schwab Foundation said. "I am confident this trend will only continue to grow in the future, and the World Economic Forum is proud to be at the forefront of catalyzing partnerships among these stakeholder groups for social and environmental change."

Who better to help bring together the often incongruent cultures and approaches of private business, governments, and NGOs than Bill Clinton? Since leaving office in January 2001, Clinton has been a tour de force on the global stage. The Clinton Foundation is an operating nonprofit. It does not invest the money it raises into other organizations but rather supports its diverse portfolio of work.

The foundation works in four broad issue areas: climate change, economic development, girls and women, and global health and wellness. Nine different initiatives help them to solve problems in their issue areas of focus. From involvement in social entrepreneurship to public health, the Clinton Foundation has successfully bridged divides across the globe. Its ever-growing community has now made over 3,400 commitments to action pledges that will impact over 400 million people in more than 180 countries.

"Wealth," Andrew Carnegie wrote, "is not to feed our egos but to feed the hungry and to help people help themselves." The Kickstarters are carrying on this tradition. Like the reboot of capitalism, they've changed philanthropy and along the way have been a liberating force for social entrepreneurs.

The Kickstarters take on problems on a global scale. Most of their work is centered on changing the lives of those at the bottom of the pyramid. As a collective they provide capital, strategy, contacts, and the imprimatur of prestige upon the social entrepreneurs that they engage.

That takes us to the next level of this ecosystem, to the social entrepreneurs themselves. They are the ones on the ground, sleeves rolled up, guided by an unquenchable thirst to repair the world in new and innovative ways. The work is daunting. The challenge is great. But there is no greater reward than the work they do. Like Carnegie before them, they are doing something for their world, and no work could possibly provide greater satisfaction.

# one for one and one for all

*We are now faced with the fact that tomorrow is today.*
*We are confronted with the fierce urgency of now.*
*In this unfolding conundrum of life and history,*
*there "is" such a thing as being too late. This is no*
*time for apathy or complacency. This is a time*
*for vigorous and positive action.*

—MARTIN LUTHER KING JR.

Social entrepreneurship today builds upon the legacy of the civil rights movement. Dr. Martin Luther King Jr. beseeched his followers that change cannot wait. He implored them with the "fierce urgency of now." Gallant leaders like King fought for equality, opportunity, and justice.

Their mantle is now carried by social entrepreneurs who seek the same ends. Social entrepreneurs based in America have taken on the great challenges of today. They are seeking solutions to problems at home and aboard. And they are doing it with the fierce urgency of now.

There are many ways to get involved in the social entrepreneurial ecosystem. Social entrepreneurship is not limited to the developing world. It is a global movement. In the developed world social entrepreneurs can take aim at societal problems at home or abroad. They've established companies that provide aid in Darfur or even next door.

How do they do it? The for-profit space uses consumer markets to power change at home and abroad. The nonprofit sector develops innovative programming and partnerships to deliver lasting and meaningful results. They all rely on The Great Convergence.

And when it all comes together, the results can be extraordinary.

That's what happened in 2006. It was a big year for social entrepreneurship. Several academic journals published important pieces on its potential. By that time it had left the distant shores of the developing world. More and more social entrepreneurs were operating in the developed world, using our consumer markets to foster change.

The one-for-one model soaked up all the headlines. It was simple. The pitch went something like this: You buy X, we do Y. No company came to embody this model—its strengths or its shortcomings—like TOMS Shoes.

For many Americans the first exposure to TOMS came through a commercial. The 30-second spot ran in April 2009. It was the first time AT&T profiled a real customer in their long-running "more bars in more places" ad campaign. Even though consumer attention spans remain undeniably short, the commercial was such a hit that AT&T then green-lit a 60-second version. It was May 5, 2009. Season eight of *American Idol* was well underway and more than 23 million people tuned in that night. During a commercial break, AT&T aired the 60-second version and, as they say, the rest is history. TOMS Shoes saw an instant spike in business, going from 9,000 visitors a day on their website to 90,000.

Here's what the ad says:

> *My name is Blake and I'm the chief shoe giver at TOMS shoes. I operate my entire business from my phone. I need a network with great coverage because for every pair of shoes we sell, we give a pair away to a child in need. It would be impossible to do this without a network that works around the world.*

The visual, audio, and emotional crescendo comes on the words ". . . because for every pair of shoes we sell, we give a pair away to a child in need." It's a touching ad and made all the more significant because it is true.

What was so powerful about the ad? Why did it strike such a chord with Americans? It had to do with the message and the messenger. The ad featured the founder of TOMS Shoes, Blake Mycoskie, who single-handedly redefined social entrepreneurship in America.

Mycoskie is one of those people who just breathes entrepreneurship. He started his first venture, a laundry business, while in college. He then started an advertising company that he sold and pursued other ventures as well. Mycoskie had what turned out to be one of his 15 minutes of fame as a contestant on the CBS reality show *The Amazing Race*.

During a trip to Argentina, Blake met women who were collecting shoes to give to children so they could meet the school dress code. That conversation spurred Mycoskie into thinking more deeply about how he could help these children and more. He came up with a plan that centered on a single, elegant solution. He would start a shoe company and for every pair he sold, he would donate one to a child in need.

With its unique one-for-one model, fun branding, and stylish shoes, TOMS was a hit with customers. "The one-for-one model I have found is really effective in allowing a consumer to know exactly what's going to happen. There is no ambiguity; there's no crazy accounting. You buy a pair of shoes; we give a pair of shoes to a child in need," he said.

By 2013, the company had given away its 10 millionth pair. That of course means it had also sold its 10 millionth pair.

As an added benefit Mycoskie noted, "When you incorporate giving into your business, your customers become your marketers. We spend very little money on advertising and marketing."

The company simply exploded and is on the way to unicorn status (that's a $1 billion valuation in startup-speak). In 2014, the company hit a valuation of $625 million and sold a 50 percent interest to Bain Capital.

With more than 10 million pairs donated and a company valuation of over $600 million, TOMS was the embodiment of social entrepreneurial excellence. They did well for their company while at the same time doing well for society at large. Or did they?

In the world of international development, TOMS spent years at the center of conversation, and not for the right reasons. Writing in *The New York Times*, Adriana Herrera of Fashioning Change said, "Rather than solve the root cause of why children don't have shoes, TOMS has created a business model that actually needs poor children without shoes in order to sell its shoes. Those children are an essential part of the company's marketing." In this same article TOMS admitted that it is "not in the business of poverty alleviation."

NYU Economics professor William Easterly, a noted critic of the TOMS model, tweeted this in 2012:

> TOMS shoes Buy-1-Give-1 keeps surpassing its own record as worst charity in development.

Other important voices in international aid, including the well-respected Saundra Schimmelpfennig, chimed in as well: "Haiti doesn't really have a shortage of shoes. There are piles and piles and piles for sale (new and used) on practically every street and side street around here."

"At worst, it promotes a view of the world's poor as helpless, ineffective people passively waiting for trinkets from shoe-buying Americans," Vox Media declared. "While the shoes themselves

---

### ANOTHER SOLE MAN

"You will never hear me call myself a social entrepreneur. I despise the word. I think it's silly," Tal Dehtiar told *Entrepreneur* magazine. He may not agree with the term (then again, there's no uniform definition anyway), but we can all agree that Dehtair's shoe company, Oliberté, is truly remarkable.

Oliberté makes trendy shoes in Addis Ababa, Ethiopia. One hundred ten employees work out of a fair trade–certified factory, the first fair trade factory in the footwear industry. All of the shoe components—leather, rubber, insole labels, and tags—are sourced from African countries. It would be far more cost effective to produce the shoes anywhere else in the world. There are an abundance of issues that make it a challenge to operate a new business from a developing nation. But Dehtair wouldn't have it any other way. He sees this as a far better model than charity. His workers have dignity and pride; they don't need or want handouts. They want to work, they want to send their children to school, and they want a better future for their family.

Profits from each sale are reinvested back into the company so it can hire more workers and increase production. In 2015, the company hit profitability for the first time. Selling online and in select retail stores, its business is growing while changing the lives of its Africa-based employees.

---

probably won't lead to any kind of disaster, that worldview can lead to bad policies and real, serious harm."

So on one hand you have a growing, thriving company that is giving away shoes. But on the other hand you have the social mission. Is it really working?

This gets back to the root of what social entrepreneurs do. They really don't just give away stuff. That hasn't worked. Social entrepreneurs go deeper to solve the heart of the problem.

It would have been easy for TOMS Shoes to ignore the critics. A lot of successful companies have critics and there are PR professionals who help keep them at bay. But TOMS did something else. They listened.

In the fall of 2013, Mycoskie decided to change course. "If you are really serious about poverty alleviation, our critics said, then you need to create jobs," he wrote. "At first I took that personally, but then I realized that they were right."

Mycoskie decided to take aim at the underlying issue behind why people would need donated shoes in the first place: poverty. The way he saw that, the best way to alleviate poverty would be through education and jobs.

TOMS built shoe-manufacturing facilities in places like Haiti, Ethiopia, and Kenya. Over 700 jobs have been created to date. They've teamed up with giving partners and launched programs beyond their traditional one-for-one model. The company has moved to tackle clean water, vision, safe birthing, and bullying. Staying true to their for-profit social entrepreneurial roots, for each expanded social benefit there is a new product to offer to consumers.

## OUT OF SIGHT

TOMS eyewear delivers not only free eyewear to those in need, but also an eye exam along with surgery and medical treatment when required. TOMS Roasting Company, launched in 2014, provides a week's supply of clean water to a person in need. A TOMS Bags purchase secures materials and training so health-care workers can deliver babies safely. TOMS StandUp Backpack funds programs here in the U.S. to combat bullying. On the newly launched TOMS Marketplace, social entrepreneurs can sell their products to TOMS' vast customer base.

TOMS went for a more holistic approach to servicing the developing world. TOMS Roasting Company acquires its coffee from small plantations in places like Peru, Malawi, Rwanda, Honduras, and Guatemala. According to Mycoskie: "I think once people understand the impact they can make buying a cup or bag of coffee, it will create an even stronger connection to TOMS than they might have already had. And that's what business is about." They haven't abandoned their original one-for-one model, but they've listened to the criticisms and made adjustments.

TOMS has also spawned a cottage industry of one-for-one companies. Soapbox, Good Spread, Out of Print, Smile Squared, Baby Teresa, and BOGO Bowl are just a few firms that have followed in TOMS' footsteps. And then there is Warby Parker.

Five years after its 2010 founding, Warby Parker already achieved unicorn status. You would have to be a little, well, crazy to start an eyewear company. Many industries have dominant established players. Almost none have the kind of rock-solid impenetrable dominance of Luxottica.

Coming as close as you can today to a full market monopoly, Luxottica controls over 80 percent of the eyewear market. They own Oakley, Oliver Peoples, Persol, and Ray-Ban. They make eyewear for Burberry, Dolce & Gabbana, Chanel, Coach, Ralph Lauren, and Versace, among others. When it comes to retail, they have a lock on that as well. They own Lenscrafters. They own Pearle Vision. They own Sunglass Hut. With more than 7,000 retail locations and 80,000 employees, they are the British Empire of the eyewear industry. The sun never sets on sales at Luxottica.

Warby Parker plays the role of American Colonist against the world domination of Luxottica. But how do you compete? Warby Parker has adopted a similar strategy to that of the Continental Army. They fight on their terms.

This means designing everything in-house rather than through a third party. This means everything is sold in-house and not by a brick-and-mortar retailer. There are no licensing deals with Target Optical (owned by Luxottica), Sears Optical (owned by Luxottica), or Alain Mikli (owned by, well, you know who).

It also means standing up for a new set of ideals and principles. Warby Parker doesn't only make awesome glasses that cost under $100—they also support the work of nonprofits like VisionSpring. Although their Buy a Pair, Give a Pair model may sound similar to the initial flaws in the TOMS Shoes concept, it is executed in a way that provides a wonderful example for other future social entrepreneurs.

Here's how it works. The company tallies up the number of glasses they sell, and a monthly donation is made. Those funds cover the cost of sourcing that same number of glasses and selling them at reduced cost to resellers in the developing world. Warby Parker's nonprofit partner then goes about training men and women how to give eye exams and how to sell glasses at very reasonable prices.

The first question that always comes up: Why not just give glasses away? By now, I hope you know the answer. That model just doesn't work.

For years it was popular for people to donate their used glasses so they could be given out to people in need. It sounds wonderful, and the people making the donation have the very best of intentions. However, a 2012 study found that only 7 percent of all donated glasses are in proper condition to be reused. The cost of acquiring, inspecting, and distributing those glasses roughly came out to $20 per item. But VisionSpring could deliver a new pair of glasses for a small fraction of that cost. It's not only about matching the right person with the right prescription (which is challenging), it also involves the look of the glasses. People should feel dignified. With the wrong pair of glasses on, it can cause embarrassment, even shame. VisionSpring's brilliant leader, Jordan Kassalow, learned this over 25 years ago when a legally blind woman returned a pair of free recycled glasses to him because of their ridiculous design.

It turns out people want choice; they want a say in how they look. And they will pay for it. Yes, even at the BoP. VisionSpring has found that a BoP consumer is willing to pay up to 10 percent of their monthly income for the benefits that come with glasses. As Warby Parker states, "More importantly, it forces our partners to offer glasses that people actually want to buy: glasses that fit with local styles, look good, work well, and make the wearer feel incredible."

Warby Parker's donations also provide jobs. A new army of eyewear sellers and eye exam providers go forth into their communities as a result of the job training program. Through their partnership with VisionSpring, over 18,000 people in more than 35 countries have received this training to date. So instead of handing out something for free that probably won't do much good, Warby Parker is helping to drive employment, economic output, and dignity in the developing world.

Warby Parker's advancement has not pushed Luxottica to its Yorktown. Nor does it have to. If Warby Parker can succeed in the face of such an entrenched market player, is there any industry impervious to the power of social entrepreneurship?

Beyond its ability to facilitate change in the developing world, social entrepreneurship is powering change right here at home, too. Our needs are different, but the approach is the same. Social entrepreneurship extends to all corners of the world. It may even be thriving around the corner from where you live.

The explosion of diabetes and obesity in America present serious public health challenges that have a direct impact on our economy. Approximately $425 billion is spent annually on diagnosing and treating diabetes patients. The estimated reduction in annual productivity stands at over $70 billion, according to the American Diabetes Association. With almost 10 percent of the U.S. population now afflicted, this has become nothing short of an epidemic. More people now die from diabetes-related illnesses each year in America than breast cancer and complications from HIV combined.

Sedentary lifestyles, coupled with sugary drinks (super-sized in many cases) and an unhealthy diet, have coincided with the growth in both diabetes and obesity. Today Americans consume more sugar, Omega-6 fatty acids, and processed foods than ever before. The biggest culprit of that consumption comes from the fast-food industry. Fast-food producers have had three advantages to more healthy competitors: price, geography, and education.

Fast foods have always been cheap. It's one of their biggest draws. They'll serve you breakfast, lunch, and dinner, and all three meals combined can cost you as little as $5. You can get a Sausage McMuffin® for $1. You can get a McDouble® for $1. You can get a sausage burrito for, well, you know, $1. For just under $5, you can get the holy grail of burgers, the Big Mac®. It comes with two all-beef patties, special sauce, lettuce, cheese, pickles, onions, on a sesame seed bun. Let's face it, hard to beat that value. But it does come with a cost to your health: The Big Mac® contains 593 calories and 33 grams of fat.

Fast food is highly accessible. There are 232,000 fast-food establishments in the United States and over 500,000 of them worldwide. Kids between the ages of 6 and 14 will eat fast food more than 157 million times per month.

The fast-food industry uses marketing to educate its customers on the virtues of the product. Annually they spend almost $5 billion on advertisements. McDonald's alone spends about $1 billion, making it the restaurant industry's biggest marketer. It works. Some 96 percent of school-aged children can identify the image of Ronald McDonald. The only figure to rank higher is Santa Claus.

There have been many attempts to combat the three-headed monster of price, access, and education that has led to the dominant market position of the fast-food industry. They have all yielded mixed results at best. At worst, it has helped to calcify the fast-food industry's vice grip on the American consumer.

Here we have an underlying social problem: unhealthy diets that contribute to a strain on the health-care system and produce unnecessarily sick citizens. Sounds like a problem for a social entrepreneur. Cue Gunnar Lovelace.

# LOVE IT

Lovelace is right out of central casting. He has a Tony Robbins–like aura about him. Perhaps it's his height or the way he speaks. Lovelace commands attention. He's a serial entrepreneur who has started and sold several companies and launched two nonprofits.

Lovelace doesn't have a traditional background. He was raised in a hippie commune in Ojai, California. At times he lived for months on nothing but rice. Raised by a single mom until she remarried a man who ran a healthy-goods club, he got an early education in the business of healthy food.

In 2014, Thrive Market launched. Cofounded by Lovelace, Nick Green, Sasha Siddhartha, and Kate Mulling, the company seeks to rebuff the price, geography, and education conundrum other healthy-food operations face. The stakes couldn't be higher. "We are at an inflection point as a species," Lovelace told me.

So how do they do it? It works like this. Users register on Thrive's site and get a free 30-day trial. To complete membership they pay $59.95 a year to join the exclusively online Thrive community. This is similar to the model used by Costco and Sam's Club. But there is a twist. For every membership purchased, Thrive Market donates one to a family in need.

As a result, Thrive engages with two different customer bases. Its subscribers are likely to be LOHAS (lifestyles of health and sustainability) consumers. This segment of the market is actively looking for healthy products and is a natural fit for Thrive. Its non-paying members (they still pay for the products on the site just not the membership) are more likely to be fast-food consumers. For them, Thrive looks to be a healthy alternative by taking on price, geography, and education.

The 25 to 50 percent off retail prices helps consumers with less disposable income enter the healthy marketplace. Thrive's distribution network enables it to deliver the ordered food quickly, usually within two days. Thrive provides educational videos and materials to users who receive the free membership. The goal of the education campaign is to empower the consumer. The materials teach how to read a label, how food gets processed in the body, and why certain foods are unhealthy.

Can this combat the billion-dollar campaigns of the fast-food industry? "The media economy is changing," Lovelace told me. Thrive is active in social media and uses a network of more than 100 influencers, celebrities, and bloggers who care about these issues. Together they have an ability to reach millions of potential customers.

Thrive's online shopping environment is easy to navigate and comprehensive. It isn't designed to be a clearinghouse for every item under the sun. Lovelace believes in curating an experience built around product excellence, not abundance. "We want to be a trusted, curated source that makes healthy living easy, fun, accessible, affordable, and aspirational," he told *Shape* magazine.

In its first year in business, the company has already logged 2 million users. It is the fastest-growing e-commerce company in the history of Los Angeles. Recently it completed a Series A round of funding, raising $30 million. Celebrities and thought leaders like Tony Robbins, Deepak Chopra, and Jillian Michaels are also early backers of the company.

Thrive is a great name for a social entrepreneurial company. Helping people to thrive is really at the heart of what social entrepreneurs do. How do you get the disenfranchised to thrive?

## A YEAR UP

At a time when unemployment remains high, quality public education in many urban areas remains low, and domestic issues at home undermine proper developmental growth, many of today's urban youth are trapped by a system that has failed them. But that is changing. Gerald Chertavian is proving that everyone can be a part of the American Dream. Everyone can thrive. His nonprofit Year Up demonstrates that every single day.

Year Up is looking to close the opportunity divide in America. According to their statistics, there are more than 6 million urban youths that lack access to the mainstream economy. At the same time U.S. corporations are facing a long-term shortage of 14 million qualified workers.

What if these 6 million youths could be brought back into the fold—trained and mentored to succeed in today's business climate? That is Year Up's mission. Through personal development, internships, and college credits, the enrollees are given the tools they need to succeed.

Chertavian is truly an incredible individual. He succeeded in business and made it big. When he and his partners sold their company, Conduit Communications, in 1999 for $83 million, Chertavian could have retired and lived a very comfortable life. Instead, he decided to work harder. He became a social entrepreneur committed to changing the lives of thousands of youths. "I always say, if you cut me open, I bleed urban young adults," he said. "And that is not going to change. It's a fortunate thing to know how you want to focus your life's work."

Year Up should not be confused with a charity that provides handouts. It's far from that. New enrollees, ages 18 to 24, sign a contract that tells what is expected of them. The terms are non-negotiable. Students earn a daily stipend while in the program, but they don't pay any tuition. Their Year Up is split between five months in a classroom environment learning personal and professional skills and six months in a full-time internship.

There's nothing new about a job training initiative. There certainly are many of them out there. Chertavian understands the skepticism. Why is Year Up not just another program? Like others who challenge the Charity Industrial Complex, Year Up focuses on the end result and has developed a pioneering model that is a completely new way to look at job training, education, and breaking the poverty cycle. Writing about his experience in his book, *A Year Up*, Chertavian noted: "The U.S. Government Accountability Office reports that the United States spends 18 billion federal dollars on 47 different work force development programs. Only five have been formally evaluated."

Eighteen billion plus 47 programs equals a classic government operation. That's why skepticism is understandable. Of course, part of being a social entrepreneur involves disruption. Year Up's model— no tuition, strict accountability, job training, and placing qualified youths into internships—is changing how people think about engaging disaffected youth.

If the program tuition is free, where does the operating revenue come from? Year Up charges fees to the corporate partners where interns get placed. This accounts for about half of their budget, and fundraising covers the rest. As a result, the students must succeed, for the future of the nonprofit is riding on them. "If our interns don't meet expectations, we don't expect our corporate partners to pay us. Year Up's solvency depends upon our interns doing well," Chertavian wrote.

Charging corporations fees for the interns is a groundbreaking concept. When we think of interns, the word that comes to mind is "free" labor. In a typical internship, young people take a job for free in exchange for getting valuable experience. Since the labor is free, its quality can be circumspect. But with Year Up that's not the case. Companies are paying for it, and they expect top value for their dollar. They expect well-trained, intelligent people to fill their intern program.

Unlike most job training programs that last a few days or a few weeks, Year Up is a long-term comprehensive program. As a result, they can deliver well-qualified interns to their corporate partners.

How's this for results? Eighty-five percent of Year Up graduates are in school or have a job within four months of graduation. They earn an average of $32,000 per year for full-time employees and $16 per hour for part-time work. Even during the height of the Great Recession, Year Up students were succeeding. They earned 30 percent more than those outside the program. Mark Elliott, president of the Economic Mobility Corporation, remarked to *The New York Times* that "these are the most exciting evaluation results we've seen in youth employment in 20 or 30 years—and the first to show a really substantial earnings gain."

## FIVE STEPS FOR STARTING YOUR OWN
## SOCIAL ENTERPRISE

To get started, there are five steps along the way that each social entrepreneur must undertake:

1. *Define the Problem.* What is the underlying societal problem that you wish to correct? As we saw with African Clean Energy, you've got to address the cause, not the symptom. In their case they didn't find a way to treat people who were getting sick from breathing in fumes of open stove cooking; they found an alternative to that form of cooking itself.

2. *Define the Solution.* How can you bring transformative and scalable change that will eradicate the problem? Think of the challenge that d.light faced when it first launched. Kerosene lamps were the norm, they were dangerous, and everyone used them. d.light had a defined solution (a safe solar-powered LED light), but would people buy it? It turns out they would indeed, because it perfectly solved the problem.

3. *Hire Slow. Fire Quick.* Even the most dynamic change maker can't go rogue. Social entrepreneurship is not a place for individuals to work alone toward making a difference. It takes a village of committed and dedicated people to take a venture from a paper concept to nascent startup and beyond. Important organizational decisions need to be made, including the for-profit versus nonprofit question that bedevils many startups. As we've seen in this book, there is no golden rule or one-size-fits-all solution for this question. It all depends on the specifics of the venture, its revenue opportunities, and its capital needs.

4. *Measure. Measure. Measure.* Big Data has come to social entrepreneurship in a big way. Unlike Philanthropy 1.0 or even

---

**FIVE STEPS FOR STARTING YOUR OWN
SOCIAL ENTERPRISE,** CONTINUED

Charity 1.0, today's change makers are expected to have a measurable impact on the problem they seek to correct. Measuring performance outcomes both positive and negative, intended result versus latent result, efficiency, effectiveness, scalability, and so on are all metrics in the standard toolbox of today's successful social entrepreneur.

5. *Scale.* It's great to make a difference. But for a social entrepreneur to be successful, that difference needs to have a multiplier effect. It needs to take root and grow so that the benefit is not felt solely by one cohort but by an entire community. Scale is hard. What works in isolation may not work when introduced to a larger population. But this is the struggle of the social entrepreneur. Without scale, problems go on. Without scale, problems get worse.

---

For five years I served as an adjunct professor at John Jay College. Almost all my students were products of the New York City public school system. They were a remarkably bright group. I rigorously prepared each lecture. I had no choice. If I slipped on facts or key points, the students would know it. And they wouldn't be bashful about calling me out on it.

Despite their obvious intelligence, many told me that they felt trapped. They were working through college but didn't see job prospects for themselves, and didn't know what the future would hold for their children. That's why programs like Year Up are so vital. For my former students and for all young people who have been failed by problems at home or a broken system at school, Year Up provides a breakout. It makes our country stronger by supplying employment, ending the cycle of poverty, and empowering youth.

## A DIFFERENT KIND OF ENTREPRENEUR—AN INTRAPRENEUR

As the drumbeat for social ventures grows larger, the media has adopted an "anyone can do it" narrative. Come up with a great idea that can change the world, share it on social media, create a website (with responsive design), and the next thing you know you've got a social entrepreneurial company and in six months you'll be presenting your success as part of a TED Talk.

If only that were true.

Starting any venture is hard work. Starting a social entrepreneurial venture is even harder. "One of the fallacies that the media has propagated is that everyone can be an entrepreneur," Thane Kreiner of The Miller Center for Social Entrepreneurship told me. "The truth is even in Silicon Valley, the world's most entrepreneurial ecosystem, you're lucky if one in 50 or 100 are entrepreneurs. Most don't want it."

The vast majority of people do not want sleepless nights worrying about payroll, scale, mission statement, vision, hiring, firing, fundraising, pivoting, and fundraising (again). Most people want jobs that provide them with dignity and a livelihood.

A lot of people become entrepreneurs out of necessity. To some it becomes an option of last resort, borne out of desperation. In the developing world you'll often see people start very small businesses selling goods alongside a road. That's not because they are entrepreneurial. "It's because they have no other choice," Kreiner said, while making clear that those same people would be delighted to work at a venture and receive steady pay in a dignified job.

There are many ways to get involved in social entrepreneurship without quitting your job, moving onto your friend's couch, and starting a new venture. There are many ways to get aboard this fast-moving train. In fact you can be a social entrepreneur without technically being one. You could be something else—a *social intrapreneur*.

Social intrapreneurs exhibit all the characteristics of a social entrepreneur. But they carry out their work within a major corporation. The field is still new, with the term itself being less than seven years old. Recently the field has caught fire with multinational corporations looking to capture the entrepreneurial spirit often associated with a startup.

Social intrapreneurs leverage the vast resources of a large corporation to create, deploy, and measure a socially minded undertaking. For too long the conversation about social entrepreneurship involved trade-offs; most notably, the security of a large corporation versus the nimble agility of a startup. Social intrapreneurs get the best of both worlds. Since intrapreneurship is social entrepreneurship internally at a large corporation, it does require buy-in from senior management and executives. That means a culture of innovation must be infused in that organization for intrapreneurship to work.

"Social intrapreneurs are quickly becoming the most valuable employees at many companies because they are good for the bottom line, good for the brand, and good for the staff morale," Joseph Agoada, an experienced social intrapreneur, wrote in a post on Forbes. com. "They are being recognized as key players in tackling the world's biggest problems like poverty, hunger, and the need for universal education."

"Let me say upfront that I was rooting for Goliath, not David," wrote an intrapreneur-in-residence at IBM in a blog post about the benefits and misconceptions of today's intrapreneur movement. Sure, startups are nimble and can adapt, but that doesn't mean they can make for a better entrepreneurial environment than an established company. "No matter how nimble you are, you can't birth a baby in one month if you put nine pregnant women on the job," he wrote. Nimble will only get you so far.

Large corporations have customers. Startups have each other. Large corporations have money. Startups have (hopefully) investors. And yet, the constant refrain in the media is how all disruption and innovation comes from the startup space. "It's as if these much larger and proven companies are incompetent, have lost their way, and are filled with unmotivated, slow-witted human zombie idiot robots," the intrapreneur added in his blog.

How does intrapreneurship look in action? Nick Hughes and Susie Lonie demonstrated just how large of an impact social intrapreneurs can have when they leveraged their existing contacts and relationships in the telecom industry to create and deploy a product that has changed millions of lives.

Nick Hughes had an idea; Susie Lonie knew how to execute it. Together they launched the M-Pesa program, which has fundamentally altered the lives of millions in Kenya. They did not create a startup to create and launch M-Pesa. It was not necessary. Instead they relied on the social intrapreneurial network within Vodafone and Safaricom (which Vodafone owned a large stake in), and in 2007 created a game-changing product.

M-Pesa: The M stands for "Mobile" and "Pesa" translates to "money" in Swahili. Before the introduction of M-Pesa, most transactions in Kenya were handled just like they were 500 years ago—in person and in cash. M-Pesa made it easy to transfer money using SMS messages. Transactions could now be handled remotely from phone to phone.

It is hard to overstate the impact M-Pesa has had on Kenya's people and its economy: 43 percent of Kenya's entire GDP flows through M-Pesa. It's everywhere in Kenya, responsible for everyday transactions like taxi and vending machine payments to bill paying and business transactions.

M-Pesa has brought banking to the poor. According to one study by Tavneet Suri of MIT Sloan School of Management and Billy Jack of Georgetown University, "In 2008, fewer than 20 percent of the population outside the capital living on less than $1.25 per day used M-Pesa, but by 2011 this share had steadily expanded to 72 percent." Suri and Jack observed that historically, the adoption of new technologies in the developing world tends to be slow. Barriers such as geography and poverty can inhibit product growth. "Mobile phones are unlikely to be a panacea for the complex myriad of development challenges that persist," they wrote in an article for *Slate*. "But in Kenya their use in general, and as a means of engaging in the financial economy, has been transformational."

In a country where the majority of people lack access to a bank account, yet 80 percent own a mobile device, M-Pesa has fundamentally changed the lives of millions. Mobile money has replaced traditional banking and is fueling growth in the Kenyan economy. Today, optimistic Kenyans refer to their home as the *Silicon Savannah*.

Safaricom earns $250 million a year by collecting small fees from its customers. With no hard costs like bank branches to support, this venture is not only helping the poor, but it's also improving the company's bottom line. For years banks balked at investing in the developing world. They fell into the old trap. They saw the poor as a group to be pitied. Safaricom saw them as a market. "You don't have to be greedy to be successful," Bob Collymore, the CEO of Safaricom, told *60 Minutes*.

And it all started with an idea by social intrapreneurs. The Business of Good has gone global. From the inner cities of America to the rural plains of Africa to the slums of India, disruption is everywhere. The Great Convergence has created the perfect storm for societal change.

One group in particular has been in the eye of that storm. They were born at just the right moment. They came of age at precisely the right time. There is no mistaking their ambitions or aspirations. In a nation that defines itself by comparing generations, this one is in a league of its own.

They are the Millennials. Get ready, for they may become the greatest generation in American history.

# rise of the millennials

*Youth is wasted on the young.*

— GEORGE BERNARD SHAW

On May 9, 1831, a 25-year-old Frenchman stepped ashore in Newport, Rhode Island. With his 37-day crossing on the vessel *Le Havre* now complete, he set to his task. The French government charged Alexis de Tocqueville with an important assignment. They wanted him to study America's prison system. But while conducting research to fulfill his assignment, de Tocqueville found something else. He discovered the spirit of what makes America great.

After he and a colleague published on the *U.S. Penitentiary System and Its Application in France,* de Tocqueville authored a book about American life that to this day is regarded as a classic. This book, *Democracy in America,* reads like an early guide to a generation of Americans who would come to shape our culture as never before.

Hard work. Fairness. Collaboration. Optimism. De Tocqueville found America festooned with this spirit. "It may be said that, in the United States," he wrote, "there is no limit to the inventiveness of man to discover the ways of increasing wealth and to satisfy the public's needs. . . . The primary reason for [America's] rapid progress, their strength and greatness is their bold approach to industrial undertakings."

De Tocqueville marveled at the entrepreneurial spirit that burned brightly in America. He was struck at Americans' verve. It was unlike anything he had seen before. Here was a nation filled with people aiming to better themselves and their community. It was something to behold.

Today, 184 years later, de Tocqueville's observations could easily be applied to a new generation of Americans. This generation—the Millennials, the first to grow up amid The Great Convergence— would look eerily familiar to de Tocqueville, but wholly foreign to the generations that preceded them.

The Millennials—those born between 1980 and 2000—reflect the essence of what de Tocqueville observed in the 1830s. They are optimistic and passionate about their futures. They inherited a flawed world and have a zeal to repair it that is unique to their generation.

The entrepreneurial nature of this generation is stunning. It is as if the Millennials have brought us full circle, from a society enamored with entrepreneurship during the time of de Tocqueville, to our more familiar career cycle of the 20th century, and now back to those 19th century passions. Essayist William Deresiewicz noted, "It's striking. Forty years ago, even 20 years ago, a young person's first thought, or even second or third thought, was certainly not to start a business. That was selling out—an idea that has rather tellingly disappeared from our vocabulary."

Millennials have disregarded the life and career flowchart that was so formally laid out by the Baby Boomers. Until now, there was a standard model that defined success, your place in the world, and how you interacted with giving back.

It went like this.

You go to college, a good one of course. Then came a graduate or doctoral degree followed by a job befitting your pedigree. In time you work your way up the ranks, you get an office, followed by an assistant. Along the way you save, invest, and do right for your family. And then, if you did well—really well—you turned to charity. Perhaps you start your own philanthropic organization or join the board of one in your community. Your later years turn out to be the most rewarding, as you watch the return on your social investment.

And that's the way it went. Until today.

Millennials are not keen on waiting. It isn't in their DNA. They don't wait for taxis, they take Uber. They don't wait for emails, they text. They don't wait to work up the corporate ladder, they start their own business. Millennials don't want to wait. So it should come as no surprise that they have no interest in waiting to make a difference. It is as if the generation has been hardwired to believe in the fierce urgency of now.

Perhaps the most interesting observation about Millennials is how quickly they have disenthralled themselves with traditional norms. As a result, they are challenging assumptions on youth that have been ingrained in society since antiquity.

Every generation, it seems, laments the youth of the day, from Socrates bemoaning that "they have bad manners, contempt for authority; they show disrespect for their elders," to the 1963 film *Bye, Bye Birdie*, in which the lead character's parents ask, "What's the matter with kids today?"

OK, Millennials probably take too many selfies, enjoy too much reality TV, and could talk more and text less. But compare those gripes with ones of the greasers of the '50s, the hippies of the '60s, the ME generation of the '70s, the punks of the '80s, and the slackers of the '90s.

Millennials came of age in the cauldron of The Great Convergence. By the time they neared or reached adulthood, the world was awash in crises. Thanks to technology, those crises were never more palpable.

This fusion—between a problematic and interconnected world—fundamentally altered how they saw the world and what they wanted to do about it. It was all laid bare. There was no ability for their teachers or parents to simply turn the page and conceal it.

When I was in the third grade, my class had a Chinese pen-pal. His name was Ying Li. We would write to him as a class and then a few days later, he would send a reply. Ying had amazing stories about China, and he liked to learn about America. He was my first Chinese friend. Later I found out our friendship had one problem—Ying did not exist. Since there was no real way to communicate with China, he was an imaginary character, created by our teacher. The lesson plan did work. I learned a lot about China. But I never had a friend there. At the time, there was no way for such communication to exist. But today, that level of interconnectivity is simply ordinary.

On a cold January day in that same third grade class, there was a rustling among the teachers just before lunchtime. Something had happened, but they didn't say what it was. I knew it was bad. Only later, when I got home, did I learn the space shuttle Challenger had exploded during takeoff. At the time, there was no other way for news to reach us in the classroom or library. But today, students are likely to know of a breaking news event before their teachers.

The Millennials are Generation NOW.

# GENERATION NOW

Everything is about today. The moment. The instant. The Millennials are an on-demand instant-gratification generation that has become emboldened by technology and molded by world events. So if they don't wait for anything in their lives, why should they wait when it comes to making a difference?

They shouldn't. And with social entrepreneurship, they don't have to.

Free love spoke to the hippies. Jack Kerouac spoke to the beatniks. Social entrepreneurship speaks to Millennials.

A study released in summer 2014 found that 94 percent of Millennials are interested in putting their skills to work to benefit a cause. More than half wished their employer had more programs engineered for giving back. According to a report by Achieve Consulting, a leading provider of HR solutions to large companies, "We don't study Millennials because they're a part of the culture, we study them because they're defining the culture."

Millennials are all about engagement. This fact is reflected on their unique brand of activism. In the 1960s, for example, activism was about disengagement—boycotts. Today, Millennials use the inverse approach—buycotts. "This generation will use their role as a consumer to make a point," Jean Case told me.

Some say they have become the most prized (and perhaps feared) consumer group of all time, and their habits are surprisingly different from past generations. If you want to know the impact of The Great Convergence on this generation, then consider the findings from the 2015 Millennial Impact Project. Since 2009, The Millennial Impact Project, with research by Achieve and sponsorship by the Case Foundation, has developed a compressive trove of data on this incredible generation. Here are some important takeaways from their latest study:

- 84 percent of Millennials made a charitable donation in the past year, and 70 percent volunteered for a cause.
- 48 percent of Millennials have donated to a giving campaign promoted by their employer at some point.

- Millennial employees tend to be most inspired by their colleagues and peers who are not in management. And the longer an employee is at the company, the less managers influence them to participate in cause work.
- Millennials are 44 percent more likely to volunteer if a supervisor does, *but 65 percent more likely if other coworkers participate.*
- Millennial employees are 27 percent more likely to donate to a cause if their manager does, *but 46 percent more likely to donate if a coworker asks them to.*
- Millennial employees find value in using their pro bono skills for good. Most Millennial employees volunteer between one and ten hours a year.
- 77 percent of Millennial employees are more likely to volunteer if they can leverage their skills or expertise, therefore companies should incorporate skills-based volunteering to increase participation and maximize the value of the volunteer experience.
- Millennials also want to know that their involvement means something. The Millennial Impact Project found that 79 percent of Millennial employees who volunteered through a company-sponsored initiative felt they made a positive difference.
- One of the top ways of motivating both managers and Millennials to give was donation matching: 74 percent of Millennial managers said they would be more likely to donate to a company-giving campaign if their employer matched at least some portion of their gift.

Case reminds business students that she meets, "Today you can be in any sector, doing almost any job, no matter the platform, no matter the chairs you are sitting in. There are exciting opportunities to use your skills and your main focus professionally to make a difference in the world."

Generation NOW means business. But not in the way we've become accustomed to thinking about it. This generation believes that profit and purpose can go hand-in-hand. Unlike previous generations, whose pursuits of money and excess are well documented, Millennials have far different goals. It is no longer simply about making money now. That's an extraordinary shift in thinking.

"I think Millennials realize that money as a be-all and end-all doesn't equal happiness," Scott Harrison, founder of charity: water, told me. Scott would know. Almost all of his 80 percent domestic staff members are Millennials.

Millennials are known for turning down well-paid internships or jobs in favor of an opportunity that allows them to have a greater impact. Mathew Paisner, CEO of AltruHelp, a website that connects aspiring social entrepreneurs to local opportunities, noticed that 75 percent of his applicants were willing to decline Fortune 500 opportunities to instead join his venture. It is hard to imagine Generation Xers or Baby Boomers following the same course of action.

They wouldn't. No other generation would. But Millennials are different. The pioneering CEO of Salesforce.com, Marc Benioff, is keenly aware of their unique composure. "When you look at the Millennials' value system, what Millennials want, they want to have meaning in work," he said. "They want to understand that the company they're working for is not just building products and selling products."

"We have had a chance to truly appreciate the link between the local and the global," said Alex Swallow, chief executive of the Small Charities Coalition, and a Millennial himself. "At the global level, we are more likely to have traveled abroad, to have friends from other countries, or simply to have grown up with the internet for a core part of our lives. At the local level, we are more likely to have moved away from our communities. The social enterprise and charity sectors, I think, benefit from having people like this who have an understanding of the larger picture."

## MILLENNIALS AND THE GREAT CONVERGENCE

The Great Convergence is responsible for shaping this understanding. It has imbued Generation Now with six distinguishing traits. These traits set them apart from other generations. When mixed together, the alchemy has unleashed upon us the new emperors of modern culture. These Millennial traits which have powered their central role in social entrepreneurship are: **C**ollaborative, **A**chievers, **E**ntrepreneurial, **S**heltered, **A**ccessible, **R**esponsible.

## *Collaborative*

Young people acting in a friendly, collaborative environment with classmates and colleagues to solve problems comes up time and time again when studying this generation. They thrive in an open atmosphere that encourages this kind of thinking. Millennials don't go rogue, and they don't go at it alone; they work together.

Millennials believe in themselves. But they also believe in their peers. And they will collaborate with just about anyone. Researchers Joeri Van den Bergh and Mattias Behrer noted, "Contrary to previous generations, Gen Yers [another name for Millennials] were brought up in an atmosphere of equal relationships and co-decision-making." That's a big shift from previous generations. It didn't hurt that the popular TV shows of their youth, *Blue's Clues*, *Barney*, and *Bob the Builder*, all focused on collaboration. But it's so much more than what they were exposed to as children that shaped this generation. Every outgrowth of The Great Convergence (more connectivity and technology at an early age coupled with the news of the world) created this fundamental zeitgeist shift.

This generation wants to be heard and wants to shape opinions. One executive at Dropbox told *Forbes* that with Millennials, "a new brand, service, or product is only started by the company; it is finished by the customers. Millennials are a generation that wants to co-create the product, the brand, with you. Companies that understand this and figure out ways to engage in this co-creation relationship with Millennials will have an edge."

At a LinkedIn Q&A session called "Millennials: How to Attract, Hire & Retain Today's Workforce," several business leaders remarked about the team-oriented approach Millennials take to problem solving. This means an entirely different workspace is required for them to perform at their highest potential. Since they like working with others, open office layouts are favored over private offices. White boards—even entire walls turned into white boards—are now popping up in offices all over the country.

## Achievers

Millennials are serious about academic achievement. They are the best-educated students in U.S. history. Not since the Greatest Generation (educated in large part by the GI Bill) have so many students gone on to college and obtained advanced degrees.

The number of college applications has never been higher. And the number of students taking SATs and Advanced Placement (AP) coursework in high school has grown exponentially.

This generation rues failure, but unlike Generation X, they have a quick recovery from disappointment. They don't lament failure and get stuck in neutral. They move on and find a new passion to pursue.

Ninety-four percent of Millennials believe that college is essential to succeed in life. In 2011, some 69 percent of Millennials said they would like to work for an entrepreneur. When the same question was asked in 2014, that figure rose to 88 percent.

After succeeding in the classroom, Millennials set their eyes on the office.

## Entrepreneurial

The entrepreneurial nature of this generation is astonishing. As described earlier in this chapter, Millennials have unleashed a torrent of entrepreneurship that rivals any other time in American history.

Fifty-five percent of Millennials are interested in starting their own business one day. It isn't surprising they want to take matters into their own hands: 63 percent believe that the largest barrier to innovation is the attitude of management. Bureaucracy, endless meetings, and standard operating procedures have no utility for Millennials.

According to one culture critic, writing for *The New York Times*: "Our culture hero is not the artist or the reformer, not the saint or scientist, but the entrepreneur. (Think of Steve Jobs, our new deity.) Autonomy, adventure, imagination: Entrepreneurship comprehends all this and more for us. The characteristic art form of our age may be the business plan."

Bentley University recently released a fascinating study that demonstrates just how entrepreneurial-minded Millennials have become. Only 13 percent of respondents said their career goal included rising on the corporate ladder. But 67 percent stated their goal of starting their own business. The head of Bentley University's entrepreneurial program, Fred Tuffile, said: "Millennials see chaos, distrust of management, breaking of contracts, and bad news associated with business. They've watched their relatives get fired and their peers sit in cubicles and they think, 'There has to be a better way.'"

A decade from now, 75 percent of the entire U.S. work force will comprise these entrepreneurial magnets. This will have profound implications for the future of American business. Millennials will determine its very nature and ethos.

### *Sheltered*

Since their early days, Millennials have led sheltered lives, far different from that of past generations.

While growing up, in cars, they wore seatbelts. On bicycles, they wore helmets.

Earlier generations had far less supervised playtime with friends. Once upon a time, parents didn't know where their children went, but simply expected them to return on time for dinner. That didn't happen with Millennials.

But other things did happen to them. Prior generations learned the basics of "duck and cover" in the event of a nuclear explosion. Millennials did not know the horrors of a nuclear winter, but they did become experienced hands at school lockdowns. While most of these were harmless drills, school shootings from Columbine to Newtown served as reminders of the world we were handing to them.

An entire cottage industry—child protection gear—emerged during the Millennial upbringing. As one card-carrying Generation Xer commented, "When I grew up, I didn't sit in a booster seat in the car and often didn't wear a seat belt when I was in the back seat. And

I was actually allowed to ride in a front seat before I was 9. I didn't wear a helmet to bike or ski. My dad used to smoke in the car and in the house. I walked to and from elementary school without adult supervision. My mom and dad never heard of 'helicopter parenting.'"

Yes, helicopter parent is now an official term in the Merriam-Webster Dictionary. This defines a parent who is heavily involved in the daily activities and safety of their child. Its first known use was in 1989, just as the earliest Millennials were approaching age 10. It is well documented that Millennials had the largest dose of helicopter parenting. With the watchful eye of a parent nearby, schoolyard scuffles rarely occurred, and skinned knees were attended to with the urgency of a first responder.

This sheltered environment may explain why Millennials are so close to their parents. Millennials came to know their parents as protectors, defenders, and their vanguard to the rest of the world. Since World War II no generation has had this kind of parental relationship.

## Accessible

Millennials grew up with the internet. There was never a time for them when it didn't exist. Even the older members of this generation had dial-up access. As a result, they expect internet to be available to them everywhere and anywhere.

They are the early adopters. They set up tents outside Apple stores to await the release of the next game-changing product. They adapt, adjust, and alter their technology as new hardware and software enter the scene.

According to one marketer: "Millennials simply expect technology to work, because that's been their experience. Remember the 'blue screen of death' that users would get on their PCs? And how Mac users had the dreaded icon of a bomb when things went bad? When I've made these references to Millennials, they don't even register, because the computers and devices they've grown up with essentially never crash."

And of course their passion for accessibility has no bounds when it comes to mobile. That's the environment in which they thrive. Mobile devices (tablets or phones) serve as their primary TV (they may not even own one), primary phone (it is doubtful they have a landline), and primary way to communicate with their social networks.

Yes, they spend hour after hour on social networks. Yes, it's probably excessive. But for a generation that smokes less, drinks less, studies harder, and dreams bigger, it really isn't the worst of vices.

Social networks are a huge part of Millennials' accessibility. It is a two-way street, enabling information to become more accessible while bringing together millions of other Millennials.

One recent study found that 60 percent of Millennials rely on social media for keeping tabs on current events. They are disrupting traditional models and threatening the mainstream media domination on ratings. Buzzfeed, for example, grew by 81 percent in 2014 and is now more popular with Millennials online than NBC news, CBS News, and Fox News. With so much information available on their social networks, it should come as no surprise that one in five Millennials has unplugged—they no longer have a cable subscription.

With all this dynamic change, it's no wonder companies and industries are vying for their attention. After all, Millennials do have an annual buying power of $200 billion. And don't think flashy advertising is going to win their loyalties. Only 1 percent of Millennials say that compelling ads would make them trust a brand. That's why social media is so important. It's the primary way to reach this demographic group. Millennials expect brands to be present on social networks and to engage them there.

### Responsible

When we think of teenage rebellion, we think about drug abuse, lack of focus at school, and alienation from parents. But the rebellion exhibited from the Millennials is of a different order. Neil Howe and William Strauss artfully examined this generation when they first arrived in college, in the early 2000s. They concluded, "Millennials are correcting for what teens see as the excess of today's middle-aged Boomers: narcissism, impatience, iconoclasm, and a constant focus on talk (usually argument) over action."

Millennials have a surprising respect for authority. They question it, but there's no talk of revolution that came to define previous generations. This generation takes its relationship with others seriously, particularly with their parents.

Millennials have strong relationships with Baby Boomers: 24 percent of them live with their parents. Unlike many unemployed Generation X members of the '90s, this is not due to unemployment. Many get along well with their parents and enjoy interacting with them. A recent study found that 85 percent of Millennials name a parent as one of their best friends.

During the latter half of the 20th century, violent crime among teens was up, teenage rates of abortion and pregnancy climbed, and alcohol and drug abuse reached new highs.

Today, youth-related violent crime is at an all-time low level. There has been a 51 percent drop in teen pregnancy since 1991. The amount of teenaged smoking has fallen precipitously. Drug use is down.

And Millennials aren't just taking better care of their bodies. They are also making smart decisions about their finances. Millennials are less likely to have credit card debt than Generation Xers were at the same age.

Millennials are more likely than previous generations to live within a budget. They haven't saved as much as past generations, but since the oldest members of this group are only 35, the jury is still out on that front. Eighty million strong, they are the largest generation in American history. And they are dead-set on making their mark on the world.

## A MILLENNIAL MOM

One of the most admirable of all Millennials, one whom exemplifies all these characteristics, is a twenty-something from New Jersey with 51 children. How did this happen? To find out, we need to travel to the other side of the globe.

Even for the most adventurous traveler, getting from the U.S. to Surkhet, Nepal, is an arduous pursuit. You can travel westward, connecting in Seoul before arriving in Kathmandu. Or you can travel east, and make a connection through Delhi, Dubai, or a number of European cities.

Once you've arrived in this sprawling 2,000-year-old city, an 18-hour bus ride through windy Himalayan roads will take you to Surkhet. Or if you're lucky, you can save 13 hours by catching a one-hour flight from Kathmandu to Nepalgunj Airport and then driving by jeep only four hours to Surkhet.

Surkhet's geography is striking. It sits in a valley surrounded by the foothills of the Himalayas. The Bheri River flows to the east. Its natural beauty is only dampened by its man-made destruction. A civil war broke out in 1996 that ravaged Nepal until its conclusion in 2006. During those 10 years, 15,000 people died and 150,000 were displaced.

Surkhet, like the rest of the country, looked forward to better days. In the decade since the war ended, the community has worked to restore this trading post town. Roads have been paved. Small buildings, a few stories in height, have been added in recent years. One of those buildings sits just to the north of the Karnali Highway. Standing three stories high it is a bright and cheery structure. It has large windows, and planters and flowers adorn its terraced spaces.

Fifty-one children call it their home. The fact that they have a home is remarkable. Orphaned and left on the streets, most had very little hope for a home or a future.

Today, they live in a very different environment. They receive education, health care, and most important, love. Being kids, they also get to play. They sing songs, fly kites, jump rope. The days start early. In the mornings they discuss what it means to be a citizen of the world. During the day they go to school. In the evening, after washing up for bed, they tell stories and talk about their day.

It all sounds like a typical family. But there is nothing typical about the Kopila Valley Children's Home and School or its inspirational founder.

She was always an achiever. A high-performing student, member of the student council, and editor-in-chief of her high school yearbook. During the summer and on weekends she would babysit, eventually saving up $5,000 from doing a job that she loved. Maggie Doyne was very much on her way in life.

The next stop was college, but beforehand she decided to take a gap year. With the support of her parents she decided to backpack around the world and gain a new perspective on life before settling into the rigors of advanced academia.

Doyne got more than she bargained for. After spending months in places like New Zealand and Fiji, she wanted to get back to what she loved for the next portion of her gap year experience: children. She wanted to make a difference; she wanted to work with kids but she wasn't looking to save them. She didn't know they needed saving. Then she arrived in India and witnessed child refugees of the Nepalese civil war.

"I was devastated to find out that so much poverty and suffering exists in our world, and I was angry that I was oblivious to it," Doyne would later recall.

What she saw in India was heartbreaking. But she also knew it was only half the picture. Those arriving refugees must be fleeing horrific conditions. She was intent on seeing it for herself. When a cease-fire in the conflict was announced, Doyne entered Nepal and her life was never the same.

She came across hundreds of children, abandoned, starving, breaking stones into gravel to sell for a pittance. One girl, a 7-year-old named Hima, had a particularly powerful impact on her. "Maybe I saw a piece of myself in her," she would later recall. Moved by Hima and by all she witnessed, Doyne brought Hima to a school and paid for her enrollment. That cost $7. Then she paid for her uniform so she could begin classes. That cost $8. For $15 she altered the life of this young girl. This ability to make a difference became addictive to Doyne.

Soon after she called home with a request of her parents. She wanted the $5,000 she'd saved in babysitting money wired to her in Nepal so she could continue helping the suffering children of the region. How many parents would say yes to such a request? Hearing the passion in her voice and the conviction in her heart, Doyne's parents sent over the money. With it she bought a piece of land and set in motion what would become the Kopila Valley Children's Home and School.

Today, Doyne is the legal guardian of 51 children. Three hundred fifty additional children attend school at Kopila. The days are long, as any parent or teacher knows. Much of the focus is on skill sets the children will need when they are ready to graduate. They learn vocational training, they raise their own livestock, and they are imbued with Doyne's passionate belief that anything is possible. It is her hope, her belief, that her children will become future leaders of Nepal and guide it to a more promising future. She has not just saved their lives, she is transforming the country in which they live.

When I interviewed Doyne, she was back in New Jersey. But it wasn't a social visit. One of the younger children was ill and required surgery. Doyne traveled with the baby for the procedure, which was successful.

Doyne's work is extraordinary. But is it scalable? "I'll never leave Nepal. I'm raising children. I won't build another school," she told me. And yet, in a different, perhaps deeper kind of way, Doyne's model is remarkably scalable.

"My scalability is getting other people on board and making them realize we can do this, we totally got it, and telling them what I learned," she told me. "As Millennials, we will make it really open sourced, really sharable. You should see my inbox. It's ridiculous how many 20-somethings are emailing me: 'Will you help me do this, how did you set up a board, how did you get funding?' It's amazing how many young women say, 'Oh my God, you have my dream job; how did you do it?'"

The world needs more Maggie Doynes. In November 2015, she won the CNN Hero of the Year award. As her story spreads, more and more Millennials are learning how to replicate her success, and not just with child development. "Not everyone needs to go to Nepal," she said. "You just have to find *your* something, and it's going to take all of us."

Doyne believes that social media has played a vital role in The Great Convergence and is a huge part of what has drawn Millennials into wanting to do good. "I keep telling people that it's not that things haven't been happening for the past 1,000 years, it's that now it's instant. You feel it; you have that visceral reaction. It's in front of us. That's a good thing. That's a gift. That's what's making the world smaller," she said. "Don't think there haven't been these terrible atrocities against women and girls for the past thousand years. This has been going on since before the beginning of time. It's just that now it can be snapped on an image and placed on the internet. And that's why it changes our behavior."

There's also an interconnectedness among the global challenges we now face. Even though Doyne's work is focused on children, it is part of a larger collection of issues that all need to be addressed before victory can be declared. "You can't solve the orphan crisis without clean water; you can't have clean water unless you have political stability and good government in place. You can't have lack of civil war until you have education. You can't have education until you have nutrition. There is not one golden solution. It is going to take every single sector working together and bringing this together. We're in a crisis right now," Doyne emphatically explained me. It may be a crisis, but Doyne isn't worried. "We got this." When you hear it from her, it's hard not to believe it.

Being a Millennial, Doyne has extraordinary characteristics in her DNA. She works collaboratively with local community leaders to ensure her school's success. "For the most part, there's a lot of mutual respect—they know more than I do; 90 percent of the time the local people know how to solve the problem a lot better than I do," she said. "I'm a piece of the puzzle, just one piece. We're a team of 80 people, and we have five, six people at any given time from countries around the world, but it's them running the show now."

She sets a high bar for achievement—not just for herself but for her children. Her work launching the home and school has all the markings of a passionate entrepreneur. Doyne noted how her sheltered background made her oblivious to extreme poverty. Once aware of its presence, she took responsibility to be part of the solution.

## RENDEZVOUS

Cars were always a central part of American youth culture. In the 1970s, Bruce Springsteen wrote songs that mythologized the idea of young people and cars with songs like "Racing in the Streets." Young people drove them to school and to work, they raced them, and they identified with them.

Cities responded to the demand for cars with more roads. And the more roads that were built, the more cars that followed. This more roads–more cars treadmill continued unabated. Only recently has there been a change. It turns out Millennials have no intention of being subjugated to their cars. They prefer public transportation—or even better, they prefer to walk.

Millennials have proven to be both environmentally and health conscious. Both traits grew out of the great convergence, when information became prevalent and easy to access. It should come as no surprise that the U.S. cities ranked as the most walkable are also the most attractive to Millennials. In the most recent rankings, New York, Boston, San Francisco, Chicago, and Washington, DC, comprised the top five most walkable cities. Coming in at the bottom of that list were Orlando, Phoenix, Tampa, and San Antonio. Walkable cities also have the highest rates of Millennial influx. What city wouldn't want Millennials to come and call it home? They are young, upwardly mobile, socially and environmentally conscious, and they fill jobs at large companies or create jobs by launching their own businesses.

This desire to be in a walkable bustling urban environment—as opposed to in a suburban area built around the car—is a titanic shift in generational thinking. But it makes perfect sense. The Millennials are all about efficiency and environmentally conscious, healthy lifestyle choices. For them, an urban environment offers tremendous advantages.

Hartford, Connecticut, is looking to plan for the future. The city is planning a major overhaul of its infrastructure. According to the *Hartford Business Journal*: "Hartford's future is inescapably tied to the Millennial generation and how those young professionals want to live, work, and play. The basis for the city's plans to build more housing units downtown and revamp its transportation infrastructure are based on the notions that Millennials want to live in an urban environment and have greater access to public transportation while biking and walking."

So far, the city has done a noble job responding to the wants and needs of Millennials. "We are trying to save America here," said one young entrepreneur who launched a socially conscious denim manufacturer in Hartford.

Even those Millennials who work for larger companies in Hartford are looking to shape the corporate ethos of their employer. "Members of our generation are looking for a shared sense of purpose," Michelle Cote, an employee for a Hartford-based incubator for social entrepreneurs, told the *Hartford Business Journal*. "They want to work for a place that they can feel good about in some way. They want more than just a paycheck."

Sociologists are now calling the 2000s the "The Lost Decade" for the opportunities missed, the gains not made, and the hardships we endured.

But that decade also forged the Millennials, who are rekindling the best of America. They are going to do it their way. And that is different. And thank goodness for that.

*Time* labeled the Millennials "The Me Me Me Generation." It sounded like a stinging indictment until you read the subtitle. "They are narcissistic, overconfident, entitled, and lazy, but they just might be the new Greatest Generation."

Comparing any generation to the members of the Greatest Generation is a tall order. They waited on breadlines during the Great Depression, and held the lines at Omaha and in the Ardennes. The Greatest Generation has always been held up as the generational exemplar. For 70 years they were unmatched in their fortitude and in their achievements.

Now, for the first time, a rival generation has emerged. The challenges it faces are completely different, but in many ways they are eerily the same. Both faced an uncertain and violent world, handed to them by their forefathers. Both had a strong faith that the best days for our country and for them lay in the future. And this new generation, the Millennials, has the verve to make an impact on the world larger than any generation that came before it.

One columnist for the *Los Angeles Times* recently wrote, "The current crop of young people, the Millennials, show all the signs of becoming the greatest generation in human history, surpassing the legendary minds of the Renaissance or the American Revolution or Brokaw's esteemed and very worthy WWII America."

While accepting his party's nomination for a second term in office, President Franklin D. Roosevelt looked out at the delegates and declared, "Here is a mysterious cycle in human events. To some generations much is given. Of other generations much is expected. This generation of Americans has a rendezvous with destiny."

So, too, can it be said about Millennials. For this generation has its own rendezvous with destiny.

# failuritis

*What you need, above all else, is a love for your subject, whatever it is. You've got to be so deeply in love with your subject that when curveballs are thrown, when hurdles are put in place, you've got the energy to overcome them.*

—Neil deGrasse Tyson

It's now time to take on the F-word. It's a dirty word for any new or experienced venture. But it's also necessary. Social entrepreneurs hate conversations about failure. But social entrepreneurs need to confront failure. This chapter gives them the framework to do so. With original reporting on Goldman Sachs's initial failure with social impact bonds, this chapter teaches the benefits and meaning that can be derived from failure. It also provides insight to one of the most exciting developments in the business of good—impact investing, and how it can save taxpayers' money while making a difference.

Writing in the *Huffington Post*, Jonathan Lewis of Café Impact noted: "The National Transportation Board (your tax dollars at work) automatically investigates every airplane crash so that industry-wide safety improvements occur and fewer airplanes fall out of the sky. When a social enterprise crashes, there is no post-mortem and, thus, no sector improvement."

Failure is inescapable. It is unavoidable. The very reason for the existence of social entrepreneurship is failure. A government failed. A market failed. A program failed. Without failure there would be no social entrepreneurship in the first place. Despite its critical role, many social entrepreneurs suffer from *failuritis*. This is a fear of failure. Untreated, those diagnosed with failuritis almost always go on to fail. But there is a simple yet powerful treatment prescribed to failuritis patients: Embrace it. Take that one step back. Because of failure, you'll take two steps forward and it will happen sooner than you think.

## FAILURE IS NOT AN OPTION

I'm sure you are familiar with the mantra "Failure is not an option." It comes from the movie *Apollo 13*. Legendary NASA flight crew chief Gene Kranz (played by Ed Harris) delivers the dramatic phrase while chaos ensues around him. Three astronauts are stranded on a dying space capsule. The spaceship must travel without the aid of its computer and needs to land with the same degree of power that it takes to operate a toaster. The ground crew has no idea how to bring them home. All looks lost.

Yet despite daunting odds, the crew and Mission Control meet each challenge until the ship safely splashes down in the Pacific Ocean.

The men and women charged with returning Jim Lovell, Jack Swigert, and Fred Haise home tried every other option—they never gave in to failure. NASA worked and worked until a successful option was found. So does Apollo 13 serve as a lesson for how social entrepreneurs should defeat failure?

No.

There were many reasons Apollo 13 returned to earth safely. Great feats of engineering, math, and emotional fortitude were required.

But so, too, was *failure.*

Three years before Apollo 13 launched, Virgil "Gus" Grissom, Ed White, and Roger Chaffee were conducting an important test aboard the Apollo 1 space capsule. During the test, something went very wrong. Within seconds, all three astronauts were incinerated.

As a result, the flight director, Gene Kranz, issued an order that to this day at NASA is referred to as "The Kranz Dictum." It states:

> *Spaceflight will never tolerate carelessness, incapacity, and neglect. Somewhere, somehow, we screwed up. . . . From this day forward, Flight Control will be known by two words: "Tough" and "Competent." Tough means we are forever accountable for what we do or what we fail to do. We will never again compromise our responsibilities. Every time we walk into Mission Control we will know what we stand for. Competent means we will never take anything for granted. We will never be found short in our knowledge and in our skills. Mission Control will be perfect. When you leave this meeting today you will go to your office and the first thing you will do there is to write "Tough and Competent" on your blackboards. It will never be erased. Each day when you enter the room these words will remind you of the price paid by Grissom, White, and Chaffee. These words are the price of admission to the ranks of Mission Control.*

During the Apollo 13 mission those two words—*tough* and *competent*—were etched on the blackboard of every NASA engineer.

Not only was failure an option for NASA, but it was essential—for saving the spacecraft and its crew. As a result of the Apollo 1 fire, all future Apollo spacecraft were fitted with nonflammable materials and each switch and wire was coated to prevent moisture exposure. During the power-up and landing procedures for Apollo 13, condensation covered the control panel (as accurately portrayed in the film). This water buildup would have certainly led to a cabin fire. Apollo 13 would have been lost had it not been for the failure of Apollo 1.

"To suggest the dire event of losing three brave astronauts contributing to Apollo 13's rescue seems almost ludicrous," said former NASA engineer Jerry Woodfill, "but the evidence is striking. What Grissom, White, and Chaffee contributed to the rescue of Apollo 13 makes them even more heroic than they were when they gave their lives so that men could go to the moon."

It's conceivable that the entire lunar program would have been scuttled if Apollo 13 had ended in an interstellar fireball.

As for that famous phrase uttered by Kranz, "Failure is not an option," well, it turns out he never said it. Twenty-five years later, when screenwriters were looking for a movie tagline, they invented the quote after a brainstorming session. The quote itself is nothing more than a myth.

Failure is an option. It's a pathway to success. Learn from it. By doing so, you are much better positioned to achieve success yourself.

## WHEN FAILURE STRIKES

Professor Steven A. Cohen at Columbia University has a favorite refrain he tells his students. I remember it well, as I was one of them. Sitting in his Monday morning management class at Columbia's School of International and Public Affairs (SIPA), Professor Cohen would remind us of the standards to which we hold government.

"If a private company fails, it is expected. Ninety-five percent of them fail anyway. But if a government program fails, it's front page news; it's a scandal," he said. The difference between failure in the private sector and that of the public sector is money. Only investors are wiped out when a venture goes under. Consumers may lose a product or service, but almost certainly a market replacement or alternative exists. But government programs are taxpayer-funded. By its nature government has a monopoly on tax collection. That means our money—your money—was thrown into the cauldron of wasteful government spending.

Nearly 200 million results appear in Google when you enter the term "failed government programs." The litany is endless. Each "scandal"—real or politicized—helps to erode public confidence in government's ability to create, deploy, and administer programs effectively.

Only 38 percent of Americans trust the government on domestic matters. Even more alarming for policy makers, only 28 percent of Americans trust the legislative branch of government, according to recent polling by Gallup.

If ever there was a field that could use a reboot of new ideas, it's government. But new ideas come with a price. Pushing forward a new government program and the spending that goes with it will quickly devolve into that familiar refrain of "wasteful government spending" if it fails to succeed. This death spiral leads to a lack of innovation, inertia, and ineptitude in government. But in 2012, a new idea was put forth. It leveraged private sector experience, addressed a public sector problem, and didn't cost the public a dime if it failed. In the same way that social entrepreneurs look to define underlying problems and then solve them with innovative (and often market-driven) solutions, this program had the same approach. Three years later we learned it was a complete failure. But what a wonderful failure it turned out to be.

## RECIDIVISM AT RIKERS

In New York City, recidivism among young inmates at Rikers Island correctional facility is a runaway problem without a solution. Despite the best efforts of policy-makers, the recidivism rate has remained stubbornly high. In fact, everything at Rikers has remained high. It's the most expensive prison in the country, costing $167,731 to feed, house, and guard each inmate per year, according to a 2013 report released by the Independent Budget Office of New York City. For contrast, it costs around $75,000 per prisoner at the ADX Florence Supermax facility in Colorado, where its inmate population includes international terrorists, spies, and serial bombers.

According to New York City Department of Corrections, Rikers Island had 77,141 admissions in 2013 and housed an average daily population of 11,408 inmates. While the current number of inmates is lower than it was at any time between 2010 and now, assaults, jail-based arrests, searches, and violent inmate-on-inmate incidents are well up. In 2014 alone, 995 inmates were arrested while in jail, almost double the figure from five years ago.

"For adolescent inmates, Rikers Island is broken," said U.S. Attorney Preet Bharara in 2014 upon the release of an investigation his office conducted into the prison. "It is a place where brute force is the first impulse rather than the last resort, a place where verbal insults are repaid with physical injuries, where beatings are routine, while accountability is rare." The report stated that 1,057 inmates under age 18 sustained injuries while in the jail.

Here is an example of one such incident:

> In January 2013, after reportedly being disruptive while waiting to enter the RNDC dining hall, an inmate, who was on suicide watch at the time, was accosted by a captain. The inmate sustained bruises all over his body and told investigators that the captain had "punched [him] everywhere." According to the tour commander's report, the captain's use of force was "excessive and avoidable" because the inmate presented no threat while lying on the ground.

As bad as Rikers was, the same troubled youths kept ending up back there. The recidivism rate for youths hovered around 50 percent. New York City wanted that lowered. Everyone seemed to agree Rikers was not a place you wanted to visit once, let alone repeatedly. In 2012, New York City embarked on a bold experiment to effect change at Rikers. It would cost nearly $10 million, take several years to measure its effectiveness, and no taxpayer money would be put at risk. That risk had been shifted to Goldman Sachs.

This was a first-of-its-kind experiment in the U.S. where an investment in a social impact would potentially yield a return. Goldman Sachs would invest $9.6 million into a program designed to curb recidivism among the youth at Rikers. If recidivism dropped by 10 percent, the company would get its money back. If it fell even further, the financial reward would increase to $2.1 million. Conversely, if the program did not hit the 10 percent benchmark, Goldman Sachs stood to lose $2.4 million. The remaining funds from their initial investment would be covered in the form of a loan guarantee by Bloomberg Philanthropies.

"We believe this investment paves the way for a new type of instrument that enables the public sector to leverage upfront funding from the private sector," Goldman Sachs CEO Lloyd Blankfein said at the time of the announcement.

This new instrument, a Social Impact Bond (SIB), created a vehicle whereby providing a social benefit could produce a profit. Jeffrey Liebman, the Malcolm Wiener Professor of Public Policy at Harvard, called the program "a way to speed up progress in addressing social problems, to focus attention on improving performance on government-financed social services, and to do so in a way where taxpayers are on the book only if the program works." Taxpayer ire is generally focused on failed programs that come at great cost. Now a new program would be implemented that only cost taxpayer money if it succeeded. It's a new way to look at problem solving.

## TURF BATTLE FREE ZONE

SIBs step on government's turf, but in a good way. As the organization responsible for the Rikers Island jail, New York City has tried without success to reduce recidivism. Just as social entrepreneurs stepped into new markets to solve problems, Goldman Sachs's SIB attempted to do that at Rikers and at no cost to the city if it failed. No wonder there was little talk about turf.

Former mayor Michael Bloomberg, who also happens to be the richest New Yorker, is no slouch himself when it comes to innovation. In an interesting twist, the taxpayers that the mayor represented were free from exposure if the program failed. But Bloomberg's personal foundation, Bloomberg Philanthropies, was poised to take the biggest loss of all by covering the majority of Goldman's potential loss.

So, how did they do?

Writing in the *Huffington Post* three years after the SIB was announced, James Anderson of Bloomberg Philanthropies and Andrea Phillips of the Urban Investment Group at Goldman Sachs declared: "The program, an evidence-based cognitive behavioral therapy that's been effective in reducing recidivism in many other correctional settings, did not work at Rikers Island. As a result, the program will be discontinued."

The plug was pulled on the program after a careful and rigorous analysis of its performance was studied by the Vera Institute of Justice.

Cue the cavalcade of critics.

*The program was ineffective. The private sector is no better at solving recidivism than the public sector. Goldman Sachs should stick to their day job. Government is better left in the hands of traditional policy makers. SIBs sound good on paper but in practice they just don't work.*

Those critics never came. Instead came something else: accolades.

"The experiment, financed by the nation's first social impact bond, offers a glimpse of a potential future for delivering government services. It is a future that promises more rigor in identifying failure and success in settings from prisons and homeless shelters to public hospitals and schools," *The New York Times* reported.

Andrea Phillips of Goldman's Urban Investment Group told me she wasn't surprised at the lack of a backlash. "I think one of the strengths and the reasons we didn't get a public backlash was we were very clear at the outset, both internally and publicly," she said. "And then we did exactly what we said we were going to do. With one full year of data post-release, we would have an outside evaluator come in.

It was all transparent." Goldman was clear with the public and with stakeholders what the intention of the program was and how they would measure success.

So the equation here isn't just that no lost public money equals no public uproar. The public is smarter than that. They want accountability and transparency. These are two areas where government often fails. A 2015 Pew Research Center poll found that only 5 percent of Americans say the federal government is effective in sharing data with the public.

The Goldman Sachs SIB at Rikers dove headfirst into the deep end of the pool. This was a new program (as opposed to a previously implemented one), in a violent and unstable prison setting. It wasn't until 2014 that a graphic 79-page report issued by the office of Preet Bharara detailed the depravity of Rikers.

While taxpayers were spared the bill, how could a failure like this be considered a success?

The phone calls from clients were a tip-off that Goldman Sachs was on to something. The callers were interested in pursuing this type of vehicle as an investment for themselves. The Rikers Island SIB involved Goldman's own funds, not client money. "When the program became public, we noticed a growing interest from our clients in aligning their investments with their values," Phillips said. She had first observed this phenomenon in the 1980s during the divestment from South Africa movement that swept college campuses and major institutions. But this was different. That was screening out something based on a moral objection. This was investing based on an alignment of values.

As a response to client interest, Goldman Sachs set up a Social Impact Fund. Clients could gain exposure to impact investments via this diversified vehicle, which was expected to be invested in three distinct types of projects. Fifty percent of the fund finances community development projects like quality affordable housing, health-care facilities, schools, and so one. Twenty-five percent of the fund provides capital to for-profit and nonprofit businesses that catalyze job creation and economic growth while bringing services to disadvantaged communities. The final 25 percent was allocated to investments in SIBs. Goldman Sachs seeded 20 percent of the fund's value, and the rest came from client money. The fund looks to provide Goldman Sachs clients with investments that offer a financial return and a measurable social impact.

"We'd love more competition in this field," said Alicia Glen, who was the head of Goldman Sachs's Urban Investment Group when the fund was created. "It would be great if more capital was deployed to helping figure out how to provide more access to early childhood education and keeping kids out of jail." Glen has since left the investment firm and is now the Deputy Mayor for Economic Development in New York City.

## THE FUTURE OF SIBS

It appears that Goldman Sachs will get its wish. When Wall Street sees opportunity, it seizes it. "Wall Street not giving up on U.S. Social Impact Bond," read *The Wall Street Journal* headline after the Goldman Rikers initiative failed. Bank of America, Deutsche Bank, Santander, and others are active or exploring opportunities in the SIB space.

"We are certainly not going to distance ourselves from our explorations into doing social impact bonds because of what happened here," Gary Hattem of Deutsche Bank told *The Wall Street Journal*. "This is the frontier of something."

Just how big that something is remains to be seen. No one at Goldman declared failure is not an option and pulverized SIBs. "People across the firm were really proud of the Rikers investment and proud that Goldman had been upfront about it. There was a level of receptivity to say let's think about something new," Phillips said.

If anything, interest in SIBs has only grown. Goldman Sachs is now working on three active SIB investments. They've teamed up with the Anthony and Jeanne Pritzker Family Foundation to finance an expansion of the Utah High Quality Preschool program. The goal here is to boost pre-kindergarten reading levels so fewer children will require remedial services and special education. In Chicago, the SIB will fund high quality pre-K services to more than 2,600 children in high need communities. Working with the state of Massachusetts and a consortium of foundations and nonprofits, Goldman has implemented a SIB to fund a high impact intervention program. The goal is to reduce recidivism of 929 at-risk young men aged 17 to 23 who are in the probation system or exiting the juvenile justice system. Goldman created a specially tailored payment system for each program that rewards the funders if benchmarks are hit. At the outset taxpayer money remains untouched for all these programs.

There is also the matter of tax savings. The payments made to Goldman should a SIB yield a positive outcome are less than the costs of maintaining the status quo. For example, with Goldman's Massachusetts SIB, the project's target impact is a 40 percent reduction of days incarcerated among the 929 at-risk youths. At that threshold Massachusetts would generate a savings equal to the cost of delivering services. But above that figure the savings really kick in. At a 70 percent increase in days incarcerated, the success payments due are $27 million but the gross savings for Massachusetts are $45 million. So in this instance Massachusetts could save $18 million while dramatically bringing down recidivism rates.

Learning from the Riker Island jail experience, Phillips sees the positive in the lessons learned. "We have spent a tremendous amount of time looking back to say what could we do differently," she said. SIBs and other social impact investment vehicles are using data to determine what is working and bringing different parties to the table to find new solutions.

In October 2015, the Urban Investment Group at Goldman Sachs and their partners on the Utah SIB went public with a very special announcement. The SIB's results were in. "Financial results at Goldman Sachs," *The New York Times* reported, "are going to look a little better this quarter because of the educational success of 100 or so kindergarten pupils in Utah." To the delight of all stakeholders, the independent data revealed that the children identified as at highest risk for being behind their peers were on track in kindergarten based on their avoidance of special education services. The United Way of Salt Lake announced the state had saved $281,550 in its first year.

The reaction in the media was downright giddy. "There's something for just about everyone to feel good about in Salt Lake's pre-kindergarten program," Vox reported.

Reuters noted that "the milestone marks a turnaround for so-called social impact bonds."

Goldman Sachs never came down with even a sniff of failuritis. It would have been easy to doubt, question, and even shelve their social impact bond investments after they lost millions on the first one. But that didn't happen. Today the Urban Investment Group at Goldman Sachs is pioneering ways to deliver social benefits. That's good for the company, good for taxpayers, and good for society.

In the wake of the financial crisis, the Occupy Wall Street movement, and talk of income inequality, it's only fair to give Goldman Sachs and other banks credit for their work with impact investing. Is it good for their business? When the SIB meets or exceeds its goal, absolutely. But it's not just good for business. It is good for taxpayers. It is good for society. That's something we should all be excited about. In Capitalism 2.0, profits and purpose walk together just as they do in the Urban Investment Group at Goldman Sachs.

It turns out only the Hollywood version of NASA had failuritis. NASA never had it. Goldman never had it. And neither should any social entrepreneur.

# the Gaddafi
# lesson

*Libyans picked the wrong
New York City realtor
to try to dupe.*

—THE HUFFINGTON POST

I've always had two (seemingly) competing interests: making a difference and building a business. While in college I explored these rival paths. I took a job at a prestigious law firm, and then volunteered on a political campaign when one of its partners ran for mayor of Washington, DC. I interned on Capitol Hill and then did so at a local TV station. Of all the jobs and internships I would take, none could fuse together my two interests. It never occurred to me that such a fusion was possible.

A few years after graduation I moved back to New York City and decided to run for office as a candidate for city council. Although I was only 24 years old and faced a crowded field of entrenched competitors, I proved to be a quick study and adept campaigner. As the election neared I felt my campaign had momentum and energy. On the evening of the election one volunteer felt that barring an unexpected catastrophe, we would win.

The next morning, three hours after the polls opened, the catastrophe arrived. The first report over the radio was that a small plane had hit the World Trade Center. But the story quickly evolved into something far more sinister. Cell phones soon stopped working. We drove around in a van and collected our volunteers out of fear that more attacks were imminent. Back at the campaign headquarters we watched the towers fall. The world had instantly changed.

The election scheduled for September 11, 2001, had been canceled and rescheduled for a few weeks later. When the polls reopened, there wasn't much hope for my campaign. The timing didn't seem right to elect someone so young and inexperienced. On election day, I was routed.

## THE NEXT STEP

I later had the good fortune of being hired by one of New York City's finest public servants, Scott Stringer. At the time Stringer was a member of the State Legislature. Today, he is the comptroller of the city and one of its rising stars. For four years I worked for Stringer and learned the intricacies of state government. After he was elected as borough president in 2005 (comptroller would come next in 2013),

I felt it was time for me to leave government. I had spent four years in the public sector and was now interested in building a business. Once again my competing professional interests were in conflict. They forced me to choose between the public good that comes from government work and the reward of being part of a successful business.

I turned to real estate as a career, first working for my aunt, Toni Haber, a top residential real estate broker at the largest residential brokerage in New York. I found that brokering deals, building a client base, and developing long-term business relationships were all vitally important skills that I could only learn in the private sector.

Even as I started to build a successful career, I felt something was missing. I struggled to find larger meaning in my work beyond achieving my clients' goals. But soon, achieving their goals would prove to be incredibly difficult.

The 2008 financial crisis couldn't have come at a worse moment for me. I was working on several condo conversion projects. In one building I had 22 deals in contract. They would never close. The buyers would get their deposits back and the developer would lose the building to default. I was left with nothing.

By 2009, as the full weight of the financial crisis took its toll on the residential real estate market, I was getting desperate, fast. The economy was in the tank. None of my clients were selling because prices had dropped drastically. None of my buyers could get financing because the credit markets were so tight. I showed up to work each day, but it was really just for appearances.

More and more I was missing a larger purpose in my work. My job was supposed to be the ultimate trade-off: I would make a good living at the expense of making good in the world. But now, that good living was in peril and my purpose was nowhere to be found. All this made me miserable.

## THE CLASSROOM

In keeping with my desire to create more purpose in my life (while helping with the bills, too), I took a second job teaching at John Jay

College as an adjunct professor. I taught several courses with titles like Introduction to Public Administration. After covering the information required by the syllabus, I would break off on tangents about how you could change the world, using the skills we learned in class. I loved teaching there.

My goal was for every lecture to be a powerful experience. I never took attendance even though I was told it was required. If any of my students didn't want to be there, I figured that I wasn't doing my job. But students came to each class during the five years I taught at John Jay. To this day I take great satisfaction in my reviews, both internal and the all-important online reviews posted to ratemyprofessor.com.

None of my classrooms ever had a window. I never had proper lighting or air conditioning (after I left the faculty, John Jay moved into a stunning new building that has positioned it as a 21st century school). But my classroom conditions were unimportant to me. My students were all I cared about. To this day, I remain in contact with many of them.

Throwing myself into teaching gave me something to do at my office. Since I didn't have any showings or any clients, I spent all day preparing my evening lectures. This made me look busy at my desk, which my manager liked to see. It also gave me a sense of purpose.

In August 2009, I got a lucky break. Someone I had met at an open house several months prior gave me a call. He liked me and wanted to give me a shot at renting out units in his townhouse. This wasn't just any townhouse; it was a 13,000-square-foot Beaux Arts gem. Obviously, I took on the assignment with enthusiasm.

Unfortunately, no one was interested. The showings had stalled and by the end of August, not one of the units had rented. Once again, I had no business.

## IT BEGINS

I spent Labor Day weekend searching online for jobs and was prepared to go back into government. I applied to a few places, but I never heard back. Despite my strong reviews, John Jay College wasn't looking for another full-time professor. Things were not going well.

On Sunday of that weekend I received a surprising email:

> Looking to rent a townhouse in Manhattan 9/21–9/25 for visiting Dutch delegation—do you have anything? How much per day if furnished? How many sq. ft.? How many rooms?

This was good news. My listing at 5 East 78th would be perfect for a visiting delegation. In fact, for years this very residence had served as the Brazilian consulate.

I quickly replied to this email and we engaged in a back-and-forth about the townhouse. The person who contacted me wanted to know about the size of each room, the views, and the ceiling height. So far, so good, I thought.

I was asked about the rear yard and roof deck and whether it would be suitable for a tent. A rather unusual request, but what did I care? I told my contact a tent could be installed in either location.

I then received a phone call from a woman named "Rachel." She was very curt. There was no small talk with her. She asked me about the rooms in the house, the position of the central staircase, and again the tent came up.

At some point in the conversation I stopped listing to *what* she was saying. I was listening to *how* she was saying it. The original email identified the potential tenants as a Dutch delegation. I'm no linguistics expert, but the accents on the phone clearly weren't Dutch. Why would they pretend to be Dutch? And why did they need a tent?

I was asked to email the floorplan to Rachel. Now the alarm bells started going off in my head. She gave me a Gmail address, but it was clearly not for the Dutch government—not with the words "Libyan. Embassy" in the email user name.

And that begged the question, "Who specifically will be residing in the townhouse?" There was a pause on the other end of the line. Then I was told the truth. This was for Colonel Gaddafi, as he was referred to on the call.

I am probably somewhat unique among real estate agents in that my background is in policy and politics. During my last stint in government I took classes at night and on weekends and obtained my master's degree from the School of International and Public Affairs at Columbia University. While I'm content discussing Manhattan apartment prices, I'm just as happy to discuss U.S. foreign policy.

"There must be some way we could get the entire townhouse," she said to me. Rachel intonated that the asking price was no problem and that I could even name my own fee if we could get the deal done. The Libyans were obviously worried about time. In less than three weeks, Colonel Gaddafi was to arrive in the United States, where he would deliver his first ever address at the United Nations. They needed to find appropriate housing and were prepared to pay a king's ransom for it.

Finally, I had an opportunity to make money. It was right there. I could have thrown out a big commission figure and the Libyans would have paid it. I could hear it in her voice. The Libyans needed a world-class residence for Gaddafi, and I had one. All we had to do now was make a deal. I could take this money and pay off all my debts and stop looking for a new job. This would be the answer to all of my problems. All I had to do was say yes. Instead I said something else.

"If you send Megrahi [the terrorist convicted of planting the bomb on Pam Am flight 103] back to Scotland, perhaps we can work something out," I aggressively barked into the phone.

"Rachel" never said another word to me. She hung up the phone.

It all happened so fast. Yes, I needed the money, badly. But this was the Mad Dog of the Middle East. Gaddafi wasn't just any garden variety dictator.

His government was a kleptocracy. While millions remained impoverished, Gaddafi and his family became billionaires during his thievery. Some 80 percent of all oil money flowing out of Libya's vast oil fields came to him. Several reports pegged his wealth at $90 billion to $200 billion, making him the one of the richest people alive.

In 1986, his agents bombed a disco in West Berlin that killed two U.S. military men. In response, President Reagan ordered a targeted missile strike that nearly killed Gaddafi.

Then came December 21, 1988. Flying high above the skies of Lockerbie, Scotland, Pan Am flight 103 exploded, killing all 270 passengers, most of them Americans. Years of painstaking investigation, followed by UN sanctions, led to the trial of Abdelbaset al-Megrahi, a Libyan agent who was convicted in a special court established at Camp Zeist in the Netherlands.

Megrahi was sentenced to life in prison on January 31, 2001. But eight years later, he was released. Doctors had diagnosed him with terminal prostate cancer. Under compassionate release principles in Scottish law, Megrahi was permitted to return to Libya.

In the end, he spent approximately 11 days in jail for every person who died in the Pam Am Flight 103 bombing.

This story was in the front of my mind as I talked with the Libyan government. Just two weeks before my phone call with them, Megrahi arrived back in Tripoli to a hero's welcome. There was another subtext to the release that deeply troubled me. There were widespread reports that the United Kingdom was in deep negotiation with Libya for an oil deal. Libyan officials had warned their counterparts in the UK that if Megrahi were to die in the Scottish prison, the oil deal would die as well.

Scottish physicians claimed Megrahi had no more than 12 weeks to live. It turns out he would survive almost three more years before succumbing to cancer.

So how could I then go about and take money from Megrahi's boss, Gaddafi? I couldn't. Sure I needed the money. But I also needed to stay true to my conscience.

The Libyans couldn't find anything in Manhattan for Gaddafi. They ended up in New Jersey, where they overpaid Donald Trump. I assumed that was the end of the story. I had told a few friends about my close encounter with Gaddafi, but other than that I didn't think there was much to say.

Word spread and three weeks later during the opening session of the UN, the *New York Post* called. They were doing a story on my exchange with Gaddafi and were sending a photographer over to take my picture. The next day the story ran with the headline "Get Lost, Khadafy."

> Keep on moving, Moammar. Agents for the terrorist-cod-
> dling Libyan strongman Moammar Khadafy were met with
> a strong-arm from a real estate broker they approached to
> rent a posh Upper East Side townhouse for his visit to the
> city this week. The broker, with characteristic New York
> chutzpah, told them to take a hike back to the desert.

> —*New York Post, 9/20/09*

That's how it started, and soon I became a media "get."

I spent a dizzying three days doing nothing but interviews. ABC, CNN, MSNBC, FOX News, and Fox Business News all had me on, in some cases multiple times during the day.

The blogosphere took off with the story, and more than 1,000 emails of support hit my inbox. I was even invited to speak at several Tea Party rallies. Given my own politics, I declined the offers but sincerely thanked them for the gesture.

I liked doing the interviews. It felt like a sort of consolation prize. If I wouldn't let the Libyans solve my financial problems, at least media interviews gave me something to do for a few days. But then the news cycle turns to its next story, I became old news, and no more interview requests came.

Once the media spectacle died down, I needed to figure out what came next for me. While the media was enjoyable, reading the emails people sent me was even more rewarding. I was proud to have made an impact on other people. One letter was particularly moving. I ended up framing it, and to this day it sits on my desk.

*Dear Jason,*

*My husband was killed in the Pam Am 103 bombing. He was 36 years old, an attorney with the Office of Special Investigations (the Nazi hunting unit) at the U.S. Dept. of Justice. At the time of his death our children, Sara and Joe, were 7 and 4. What you did in refusing to rent the apartment to the Libyans has made you a hero in our family. As you are probably aware, business interests (in particular oil, but also military equipment) probably played a role in why Megrahi was released. It is refreshing to know that there are some business people who have a moral compass and conduct business accordingly. There is a story in the Talmud that says in the world to come the first thing we will be asked by God is whether we were honest in our business deals. This is because how we conduct ourselves in business has a great deal to do with what kind of human beings we are.*

I enjoyed selling apartments, but this filled me with a more significant sense of purpose. I began to wonder how I could repeat this over and over again. Was there a way to integrate this sense of community and responsibility into the DNA of my work?

At first I didn't think it was possible. I certainly couldn't make a career out of rejecting dictators. But the more I thought about profits and purpose I began to consider the world in which we lived. It appeared that our culture was in the midst of a metamorphosis. A parade of problems was intersecting with a trail of technology. I had it all wrong. There were ways to integrate profits and purpose. They weren't in competition with one another. The Gaddafi lesson exposed The Great Convergence to me. From there I could see the future of business. And I wanted to be a part of it.

We have a saying in the real estate business: "Thank God for the used car salesman." In most consumer surveys, they are the only profession ranked lower than ours. (Yes, the public holds lawyers in higher esteem, although over the past year one group has fallen to the very bottom of the rankings: members of Congress.)

## LESSON LEARNED

The Gaddafi lesson shattered my internal struggle concerning working in government or working in the private sector. It no longer mattered in what sector I worked provided I could create a social mission. Starting with the premise that we would be in business to make a difference in the world was a big level shift for me. This belief became our raison d'etre. Many companies have charitable arms or causes by which they are associated. But among my competitors, none were actually in business because they wanted to improve the world.

I attended TEDActive and delivered a short talk there about my Gaddafi experience. While there I connected with new people who helped to shape my early thinking on social entrepreneurship. I had the business background and my brother Cory was a technology expert. In September 2010, one year after the Libyan government first contacted me, my brother and I launched a different kind of real estate company. This company would solve the quandary I'd had about working to make a difference or working to earn a living. It would do both, and it would be called Rubicon Property.

Our company was going to be the first of its kind in the world of residential real estate. It was going to be about . . . water.

What does a residential real estate firm have to do with water? Nothing, until we connected them. It occurred to me that housing is the essential element of living in the developed world. In the developing world, this essential element is water. My company would bring them together.

Water is the most precious commodity on the planet. It is the only one required to sustain all life. Yet unlike other commodities such as oil, water seems so plentiful there is very little conversation about it running dry. However, history shows us that control of water has been used to control entire populations.

From the days of Caesar through the Cold War to the current state of world affairs, governments have used water as a control mechanism. Whenever the tap was turned off, the implications were deadly.

Water is the most taken for granted of all our resources. Here in the developed world, we turn on the tap, open the bottle, or depress the button on the fountain and it's there for us to consume. Drinkable water is everywhere and it is plentiful.

Only it's not.

As California has learned during its most recent drought, water is a precious commodity. When it goes dry, the implications are devastating. Can you imagine your community without access to clean water? This isn't a hypothetical question for people living in the developing world. Most people are surprised to learn how many lack access to safe drinking water.

663,000,000.

Can you imagine if the United States, Russia, and Germany had zero drinkable water for their citizenry? It would be a catastrophe of unimaginable proportions. Yet that is precisely the magnitude of the clean-water crisis. The afflicted nations are places like Rwanda, Ethiopia, Somalia, and Niger—places that rarely make it on to the evening news and which most people would have trouble locating on a map.

Even a small company could make a difference in the clean-water crisis. For as little as $5,000 in funding, a clean-water well could be built and operated in the developing world. That well would provide potable water for 250 people.

In the developed world we consider housing an essential element of living. In the developing world, this essential element is water. Our firm would connect the two. We would create a real estate brokerage that was committed to helping end the clean water crisis. This gave us an identity and a new way to measure our success that would be different from our competitors. Success would be calculated by determining how many lives we had saved. Because we could only make donations to fund clean-water projects if we closed deals, I posited that the more wells we funded, the more deals we did and the more money we made.

We tracked our impact and donations made to charity: water (a perfect recipient of our donations) on our website. It was purposely put front and center as it was the keystone metric for our business.

With all of this worked out on paper, we were ready to launch our company. New real estate ventures require millions of dollars in capital and thousands of clients in a Rolodex. We had neither. On the day we started our company, we had a grand total of one apartment to sell.

I wanted people to know about us. We had no money to advertise, so I decided to try free media exposure.

I thought we needed an authoritative news outlet to write about us. Appearing in a high-profile newspaper would establish a certain level of legitimacy for our business. So with nothing to lose I pitched our story to *The Wall Street Journal*.

To my shock, they jumped on the story.

A few days later they ran an article with the headline "Gadhafi Encounter Leads Broker to Launch Firm."

The story tied together my experience with the Libyan government with my new social venture. The article was perfection. Rubicon Property couldn't afford to tell its own narrative, so instead we had *The Wall Street Journal* do it for us. A hand-sketched image of me accompanied the article.

After *The Wall Street Journal* article appeared we sat around in my apartment waiting for some validation to our belief. We didn't have to wait too long.

That afternoon I received the following email:

> I read about you in the WSJ. Very impressive and we actually share an interest in "giving back". I am interested in selling my townhouse. The house has approx. 4200 square feet. No keys to the Park, but it has a recently renovated back yard which is private, quiet AND you can bring your pet and a cup of coffee without being turned into the "Park Police".

A few days later I met with the owner. She was very jaded, and with good reason. Her East 18th Street townhouse had been on the market for four years with four different brokerages. They all failed to sell her home. Instead she was trying to sell it on her own. That wasn't going well either.

During our meeting we talked more about our company's work with charity: water than we did about the market. She was genuinely interested in our business model. After hearing so many stale broker pitches, she was hearing a fresh perspective from me.

I told the owner she wasn't on the market four times with four different firms doing four different things. She was really on the market four times with each firm doing the same thing. "Why not try something different?" I asked.

She was intrigued, but then asked me a series of real estate questions. These are the questions that typically determine whether an owner is going to hire you.

"Have you ever sold a listing that was asking over $5 million?" she asked.

"Nope," I replied.

"How about $3 million?" I shook my head no.

"OK, how many townhouses have you sold?"

"This would be my first," I replied with a sheepish smile.

At this point most brokers are shown the door. I flunked the basic criteria to get a big listing like this. But she kept talking to me. I focused the conversation as much as I could on my social mission instead of my sales record.

The strategy worked. As the owner got to know our company better during the course of the listing, she became our biggest champion. She was proud to be affiliated with our company. She told her friends and family about our social mission.

This seller wouldn't be the only one to do so. A few months later we were tasked with selling an even larger townhouse in the East Village. Soon after getting the listing we felt it was important to educate our real estate colleagues on the significance of the clean-water crisis. In the glitzy world of luxury Manhattan sales, decadent cocktail receptions are the norm. Our event would not be confused with any of those. It was a serious evening of important conversation. Although we invited a good amount of people, we had no idea if any would actually show up. Despite the cold and four inches of snow on the ground, we had a packed house. A reporter from *The Real Deal*, a powerful trade publication, live-tweeted from the event. It was a tremendous success. That owner became so enthralled with our social mission, she ended up joining our company (and yes, we did sell the townhouse, to a well-known celebrity couple for over $5 million).

On the very last day of our exclusive agreement on the East 18th Street townhouse—yes, we cut it that close—we sold it for over $4 million. I'll never forget sitting at the closing table, acting calm and collected, while my mind raced with excitement. When the check was passed to me, I stared at it for a while and took in the moment. With the commission from a big sale like this we could invest in our company and grow our business. This put Rubicon Property on the map. Even the biggest firm in New York City had the listing and they couldn't get it sold. We succeeded where four established firms had failed. It was a moment to savor.

As excited as I was at the closing on that deal, it wasn't the high point of the transaction. That came 18 months later. A series of photos arrived from Wembro, Ethiopia. A clean-water well had been installed for the local villagers. Women and children were using the well, no longer walking four miles each day to bring drinking water back to Wembro.

At the base of the well pump was a concrete plaque to note its location. In the center of this plaque was the name of the company that funded its construction.

It simply read, "Rubicon Property."

# the pale blue dot

*Yesterday is gone.*
*Tomorrow has not yet come.*
*We have only today. Let us begin.*

—Mother Teresa

It was past my daughter's bedtime, but I had something I wanted her to see. At just after 9:00 P.M. on a summer evening, we looked out the north-facing windows of our living room. Just 30 blocks removed from Times Square, the night sky never turns black. The bright lights of the big city radiate outward, blocking out the nightly view of the heavens. Only the brightest of stars, like Vega, and the brightest of planets, like Jupiter, are easily visible on a typical summer night. But it wasn't a star or a planet I wanted her to see on this night—it was something man-made.

At precisely the appointed moment it appeared. Traveling at 17,150 miles an hour, and 250 miles above Earth, the International Space Station (ISS) sailed overhead. Plain in the night sky, it lacked the flickering lights of an airplane or the rotor howl of a helicopter. Its sheer speed made up for its lack of celestial bling.

With the kind of enthusiasm that comes with being 3 years old, she waved hello to the space station. The greeting didn't last long. Moments later she bid it farewell. Its supersonic speed carried it away from us and out of view.

The ISS flies over 75 percent of earth and 95 percent of its population. It flies over pillaged forests. It flies over penniless refugees. Sixteen times a day it laps the earth and peeks down at humanity. It is one of our greatest triumphs—yet it bears witness to our worst tragedies.

## A UNITED NATIONS

Two years after its initial 1998 deployment during a flyover of the northeast, the ISS must have been amazed at what it saw. Gathered below was an assemblage of global leaders the likes of which had never before occurred.

They were all there: 100 heads of state, 47 heads of government, three crown princes, 5 vice presidents, 3 deputy prime ministers, and 8,000 delegates. Even North Korea sent a delegation (although during a stopover in Germany they got into an argument with American Airlines officials and decided to go back home). At no point in history had that many leaders congregated together for a single event.

The Millennium Summit was gaveled into session on September 6, 2000. Over the next three days the United Nations would stake its vision for the 21st century. The delegates opted to think big. They adopted a framework of goals to be achieved by 2015. These goals became the Millennium Development Goals (also known as the MDGs). In the glass-half-full era before 9/11 there was reason to believe anything was possible. Vladimir Putin, during his speech at the summit, stressed disarmament and his desire for world peace. The Israelis and Palestinians were in direct contact and Israeli Prime Minister Ehud Barak declared, "The opportunity for peace in the Middle East is now at hand and must not be missed."

The optimism of the time is reflected in the Millennium Development Goals, which were formally adopted at the summit. The following were meant to be completed by 2015:

1. Eradicate extreme poverty and hunger
2. Achieve universal primary education
3. Promote gender equality
4. Reduce child mortality
5. Improve maternal health
6. Combat HIV/AIDS, malaria, and other diseases
7. Ensure environmental sustainability
8. Develop a global partnership for development

These eight goals sought to bring a large swath of change to billions of people. Critics challenged it was too big, too ambitious, and impossible to accomplish by 2015.

So, how did they do?

"The global mobilization behind the Millennium Development Goals has produced the most successful anti-poverty movement in history," UN Secretary-General Ban Ki-moon wrote in the 2015 UN report on the MDG accomplishments.

Let's look at each 2000 MDG against the 2015 result, as documented by the UN. In each category tremendous progress was made. While more work needs to be done—much more, in some categories—there is no denying that the needle has been moved in the right direction.

1. *Eradicate extreme poverty and hunger*
   In 1990, 47 percent of those living in developing countries lived on less than $1.25 per day. By 2015, that number dropped to 14 percent.

2. *Achieve universal primary education*
   Primary school enrollment rose to 91 percent, up from 83 percent in 2000.

3. *Promote gender equality*
   Ninety percent of nations have more women in government than in 1995.

4. *Reduce child mortality*
   Global child mortality rates have decreased 50 percent since 1990.

5. *Improve maternal health*
   Maternal mortality has declined by 45 percent since 1990.

6. *Combat HIV/AIDS, malaria, and other diseases*
   New HIV infections plummeted by 43 percent, and almost 13 million more people are receiving antiretroviral therapy since 2000.

7. *Ensure environmental sustainability*
   The ozone layer is on track to fully recover from depletion by the middle of this century. Access to clean water has improved, and the percentage of the urban population living in slums fell from 39.4 percent in 2000 to 29.7 percent in 2014.

8. *Develop a global partnership for development*
   Development assistance from developed nations rose by 66 percent to over $135 billion since 2000.

These accomplishments are even more impressive when you consider the cavalcade of crises the world has faced during those 15 tumultuous years. Lost in all the bad news that forged The Great Convergence was the good work that came out of the United Nations.

The UN had many partners to help tackle the MDGs. At every turn social entrepreneurs were a part of this success story. They did it not by offering charity, but instead by offering solutions. That distinction made all the difference. Social entrepreneurs played a critical role in delivering scalable problem-solving solutions.

They did it all: from low-cost bed nets in Tanzania to IT facility infrastructure in Serbia to distributors of low-cost generic medications in the Philippines. Social entrepreneurs worked in concert with governments, non-government organizations (NGOs), and other stakeholders to achieve what many felt was impossible.

The UN report went on to conclude that the MDG agenda worked to spur global action. The second act of the MDGs was adopted in 2015. Called the Sustainable Development Goals, they contain a larger portfolio of 17 goals to tackle. The deadline for achievement is 2030, and the price tag is estimated to be $3 trillion.

Like the 2000 summit, the adoption of the Sustainable Development Goals brought out the stars of the global stage. It coincided with the opening session of the 2015 United Nations General Assembly, which in its own right has become a spectacle that combines statecraft with stagecraft. Once again, the leaders of the world congregated for the summit. But this time something was different.

The session began with Pope Francis delivering opening remarks before the goals were formally adopted. "A selfish and boundless thirst for power and material prosperity leads both to the misuse of available natural resources and to the exclusion of the weak and disadvantaged," Pope Francis told those assembled. "Any harm done to the environment, therefore, is harm done to humanity."

Setting an unmistakably optimistic vision for what can be, the UN Secretary-General Ban Ki-moon told the assembled group: "The new agenda is a promise by leaders to all people everywhere. It is an agenda for people to end poverty in all its forms—an agenda for the planet, our common home."

Even with Vladimir Putin no longer talking of peace, and the Israelis and Palestinians no longer talking, there was a palpable feeling that the world had an opportunity to take a major step forward. It was now 70 years since the UN held its first session, when the world was rebuilding from a world war and trying to navigate the Cold War. Its original charter was dedicated to "We the Peoples"—a statement of belief that we are all interconnected. True to that charter is the agenda laid out by the Sustainable Development Goals (SDGs).

Something else was different this time around, too. This time it wasn't just world leaders and policy-makers that gathered for the United Nations Sustainable Development Summit. Like they were seeing a rock band on a reunion tour, a crush of fans—yes, fans—took New York by storm to be a part of the event. They came from all over the country—thousands of people who don't work in government or for an NGO. But for them there was no place else they would rather be.

When leaders gathered for the 2000 summit, it was a backroom affair. The diplomatic community was hermetically sealed inside their own bubble. But The Great Convergence burst that bubble, and now such gatherings had become an event for everyone.

A series of events built around the opening of the General Assembly provided ample opportunity to make the most out of the week. Scott Windes, a graphic designer from Utah, commented: "It's the greatest thing ever. You get fascinated with these people who are doing their part to make a difference." While in New York he attended the Global Citizen Festival and took classes on a variety of issues.

Outside the glittering Manhattan hotels that housed foreign dignitaries, people waited breathlessly hoping for a glimpse, handshake, or even better, a selfie with a world leader. Tony Blinken, the deputy secretary of state, and Helen Clark, the administrator of the UN development program, had people waiting in line to take selfies with them. It's doubtful they'd experienced that before.

The Social Good Summit had 1,800 participants. Now in its sixth year, it grows larger and larger. Pete Cashmore, the founder of Mashable who helped organize the summit, along with the UN Foundation, the 92nd Street Y, and the UN Development Programme, told *The New York Times*: "It's about turning UN week inside out. Rather than a few powerful people deciding the fate of the world, how do we get everyone involved and engaged in a dialogue?"

Actors, activists, educators, reporters, and officials spoke at the Social Good Summit. The event hashtag, #2030NOW, collected more than 1.6 billion impressions on Instagram and Twitter. For two days an important dialogue took place on how to use technology and new media to unlock social good initiatives.

"The SDGs are a shift in the paradigm for international development," Sarah Hearn, associate director and senior fellow at NYU's Center on International Cooperation, told the Council on Foreign Relations. "The MDGs were about resource transfer from rich countries. The SDGs are universal—they're supposed to apply to all countries and try to overcome the 'West lecturing the rest' dynamic."

Immediately critics pounced. They called the SDGs overly broad and expensive. It was a replay of the criticisms of the MDGs in 2000, which proved to be unfounded. Once again social entrepreneurs will be called upon, and once again they will answer the call.

This glorious week in Gotham revealed the impact of The Great Convergence, the power of Capitalism 2.0, and the potential of the Business of Good. If the SDGs achieve their lofty aims, we will have reached a point of no return. Mankind will have finally, after 3,000 years of history, achieved something never before thought possible. We will have crossed the Rubicon, all of us.

## CROSS THE RUBICON

The general approached the Rubicon River. It wasn't much to behold. Shallow, craggy, and narrow, it had never been more than a minor waterway. The Rubicon flows along the Apennine Mountains until it reaches its terminus in the Adriatic Sea. But this river was not important for its geographic importance. It had a special symbolic value. That's why the general was here. For what was about to be done was more than just dangerous. It was treason. Julius Caesar was about to cross the Rubicon.

The evening before the act was to take place he attempted to keep up appearances so no one would grow suspicious. He took a tour of a fencing school that he himself had proposed, he viewed public games, and then, as was his ritual, he had dinner with a large group of friends. He did not hint at what was to come.

The next morning, January 10, 49 B.C., Caesar led his Thirteenth Legion to the edge of the Rubicon River. There they stood, awaiting the order from their general. No Roman army was permitted to cross the river and enter Rome proper. The Roman Senate and its leader, Pompey, had declared such an act punishable by death. Either they lay down their arms and disband or they cross the Rubicon as enemies of the state. Up until this date in history, no Roman army had dared to cross the Rubicon.

It was assumed that Caesar would follow with established precedent. But Caesar was not a typical man. He sought glory for himself, and at the same time, he sought glory for the citizens of Rome. He did not want to wait until later in life to make a difference. He wanted everything, right then. The booty from his conquests was quickly used to fund public shows, gladiator contests, games, and banquets. He paid for the renovation of public buildings and was known for his public works. Caesar was a social entrepreneur of antiquity.

In 49 B.C., Rome was a tempest. The Republic lacked central authority and the expansive territory under Roman control was becoming ungovernable. Treachery was everywhere, both at home and abroad. The Senate was filled with men of conflicting and compromised interests.

Rome was undergoing its own Great Convergence. Caesar looked out to his warriors and declared, *"Alea iacta est"*: The die is cast.

In defiance of the status quo, Caesar crossed the Rubicon. With his act of insurrection now underway, he had reached a point of no return. He would conquer Rome or he would be vanquished trying.

For Julius Caesar, this was the first step in his eventual coronation as *dictator perpetuus*—dictator for life. History would record him as one of the most successful generals and controversial leaders of all time. But it all started with his journey across the shallow waters of the Rubicon—that point of no return. We can only wonder how history would be different if Caesar had instead acquiesced, disbanded his army, and meekly return to Rome.

Caesar made a choice. He chose to conquer.

"Crossing the Rubicon" has since become a metaphor for engaging in a point of no return. It also perfectly describes the social entrepreneurial movement of today.

It is a point of no return for capitalism. It is a point of no return for consumers. This fundamental shift in thinking cannot be undone. The genie cannot be put back in the bottle. It leverages a new set of values in a world reborn. It changes the very definition of success and elevates purpose to be on par with profits. Social entrepreneurship is altering the rules in business. A focus on short-term shareholder returns has been replaced with a consideration for long-term stakeholder outcomes.

Successful social entrepreneurs will cross their own Rubicon River. They approach it just as Caesar did, with careful consideration. They review their options. They weigh their risks. They might even have dinner with friends before acting. And if they are ready for the journey, they cross the river.

By doing so, social entrepreneurs avoid falling victim to the enemy: inaction. With so many challenges before us, our greatest folly would be to wave the white flag of surrender. Or worse, to assume that a no-win situation is inevitable. Social entrepreneurs fail to subscribe to this notion.


## THE *KOBAYASHI MARU*

Social entrepreneurship is our best chance for a more prosperous and a more peaceful future. It knows no political ideology. It is agnostic to religion. It's about all of us who occupy the 196.9 million square miles of Earth. We are faced with very big challenges. Some claim we are in a no-win situation and we must simply make the best of it.

*Star Trek* fans are familiar with the *Kobayashi Maru* simulation. Each Starfleet cadet is required to undergo this test of character. In the simulation a cadet is presented with a crisis. The *Kobayashi Maru*, a

Starfleet vessel, is stranded in enemy Klingon territory. The cadet can chose to abandon the *Kobayashi Maru* and leave its crew to die or it can attempt a rescue, violate the Neutral Zone, and risk all-out war. If a cadet elects a rescue mission, enemy ships quickly appear and destroy the rescuing ship, thus ending the simulation.

In the history of the Starfleet Academy, only once did a cadet successfully rescue the crew. His name was James T. Kirk. Rather than play in a rigged game, he changed the rules. By reprogramming the simulation he was able to save the ship and not be destroyed. Kirk later explained that he did not believe in the no-win scenario. Starfleet gave him a commendation for original thinking.

That is what social entrepreneurs do. They change the rules of the game. They don't believe in the no-win scenario. They use original thinking to bring new solutions to the table. At a time when the Doomsday Clock sits just three minutes to midnight, we remain in desperate need for more change makers to refuse to believe in the *Kobayashi Maru*.

## THE BIG PICTURE

We think the world is so big, its population so dense, and its urgent needs so great. But perhaps the most insightful way to consider it is to look at ourselves from afar.

On Valentine's Day 1990, from 3.7 billion miles away, the space probe Voyager 1 focused its camera back on us and took one of the most remarkable images of all time. Known as the Pale Blue Dot, it shows Earth as a minor, insignificant speck in the cosmos. Some 640,000 individual pixels comprise the image, yet Earth makes up only 12 of those pixels.

Astronomer Carl Sagan, reflecting on the meaning of the image, wrote this in his 1994 book, *Pale Blue Dot*:

> *From this distant vantage point, the Earth might not seem of any particular interest. But for us, it's different. Consider again that dot. That's here. That's home. That's us. On it everyone you love, everyone you know, everyone you ever heard of, every human being*

*who ever was, lived out their lives. The aggregate of our joy and suffering, thousands of confident religions, ideologies, and economic doctrines, every hunter and forager, every hero and coward, every creator and destroyer of civilization, every king and peasant, every young couple in love, every mother and father, hopeful child, inventor and explorer, every teacher of morals, every corrupt politician, every "superstar," every "supreme leader," every saint and sinner in the history of our species lived there—on a mote of dust suspended in a sunbeam.*

*The Earth is a very small stage in a vast cosmic arena. Think of the rivers of blood spilled by all those generals and emperors so that in glory and triumph they could become the momentary masters of a fraction of a dot. Think of the endless cruelties visited by the inhabitants of one corner of this pixel on the scarcely distinguishable inhabitants of some other corner. How frequent their misunderstandings, how eager they are to kill one another, how fervent their hatreds. Our posturings, our imagined self-importance, the delusion that we have some privileged position in the universe, are challenged by this point of pale light. Our planet is a lonely speck in the great enveloping cosmic dark. In our obscurity—in all this vastness—there is no hint that help will come from elsewhere to save us from ourselves.*

*The Earth is the only world known, so far, to harbor life. There is nowhere else, at least in the near future, to which our species could migrate. Visit, yes. Settle, not yet. Like it or not, for the moment, the Earth is where we make our stand. It has been said that astronomy is a humbling and character-building experience. There is perhaps no better demonstration of the folly of human conceits than this distant image of our tiny world. To me, it underscores our responsibility to deal more kindly with one another and to preserve and cherish the pale blue dot, the only home we've ever known.*

It is our responsibility to bring peace to the pale blue dot, to protect its inhabitants, to preserve its future. It is all we have. This tiny speck of light and life is ours alone. You've read about social entrepreneurship, how it came to be, what it is today, and what it means for us tomorrow. It is our best chance—maybe our last chance—for a brighter future.

Is the Pale Blue Dot worth it? Are you?

After the ISS passed us by, it was my daughter's bedtime. Warm under her blanket, she soon fell asleep. I know she can sleep well at night. For when the dawn breaks, social entrepreneurs will return to their business, the Business of Good. They'll cross the Rubicon. They'll save the *Kobayashi Maru*. They'll blossom on the Pale Blue Dot.

And we are all better off for it.

# acknowledgments

On July 30, 2015, I received a call from my literary agent. After months of searching for a publisher, the incredible team at Entrepreneur Press was ready to sign me to a book deal. The only challenge would be the delivery date. The publisher wanted me to complete the manuscript by early November.

I assured my literary agent this would not be a problem. Despite my busy work schedule, I was confident I could do the writing at night and on weekends. There would be no distractions from the task ahead of me.

As a long-suffering New York Mets fan, I've grown accustomed to their summer swoon into baseball irrelevance. In late July they were fading on schedule. It appeared I wouldn't be missing much by hunkering down and writing my book instead of watching their games. The day after I signed my book contract, the Mets completed a series of trades and started a remarkable run of play. Their season didn't end on schedule in September. It didn't end in October either. By the time they lost the World Series, my manuscript was about due. Despite the Mets' surprising run, I still delivered the book on time. Being superstitious, I may start all future book projects just ahead of the Major League Baseball trading deadline.

I need to thank the many people who made this book possible. First, I have to praise the fortitude of my literary agent, Kathy Green. A year before we reached a book deal with Entrepreneur Press, I ran into Kathy at a George Washington University alumni event. I mentioned my interest in writing a book to her. To my amazement she didn't brush me off. Instead, we set up a later meeting at her office, where she politely grilled me on what book I wanted to write and why I was the right person for it. I presented her with two ideas. The first one had no chance, she told me. But the second one had potential. From there I started working on a book proposal. We made round after round of changes, created a sample chapter—which later became sample chapters—and a few months later Kathy had a proposal to pitch.

After six months of shopping the proposal, Kathy invited me to lunch to discuss the status of her efforts. Almost every publisher liked it, but as I was a first-time author, there was an extra degree of risk. There was resistance because I didn't have a large platform or track record of selling books. I was prepared for Kathy to throw in the towel. Instead, she doubled down. Kathy assured me the right publisher was out there; we just needed a little more patience. A few weeks later, on June 4, 2015, she sent me this email: "You are going to get a book deal if it kills me! But let's see what happens."

Luckily, it didn't come to that. Kathy's conviction proved its worth. Jillian McTigue of Entrepreneur Press read over the book proposal and liked it. Unlike others in the publishing industry, she believed in me just as much as she believed in the book. On our first call, Jillian said she would pitch this proposal aggressively to her bosses. It worked. A few weeks later we came to terms on a deal.

Everyone at Entrepreneur Press was terrific to work with on this project. From our very first call, my editor, Jennifer Dorsey, demonstrated unwavering support for the book. As we got underway she reminded me to have fun and to not get stressed out at the challenge ahead. Even though I had a tight deadline and tons to accomplish, I got through it all piece by piece. Jen never treated me like a first-time author. She treated me like an author, and for that I'll always be grateful. Jen also brought in the very talented Jim Markham to help edit the book, and his insights were truly exceptional.

No one was more valuable in the creation of this book than the incredibly gifted Ryan Isenberg. A recent graduate from Cornell, Ryan brought enthusiasm, knowledge, and a Millennial's perspective to the material. He became my right hand on this endeavor. His command of structure, his understanding of story, and his agility with language are on a level I have rarely, if ever, seen before. Ryan was vital in shaping the ebb and flow of the book. He listened to all my interviews and kept the project moving in the right direction. As the book was nearing completion, Ryan suggested we read the entire manuscript out loud. It took three days. But it was very helpful. I've become a believer in this approach. One day I'll get to say I knew him when . . . .

As I think back on all those who helped make this book possible, in many ways this journey for me began almost 17 years ago. After opting not to go to law school, I went to work for acclaimed author Gail Sheehy. From Gail I learned the essence of good writing. She taught me about narrative and how to build upon a central theme over the course of a book. I'll always cherish the evenings I spent with Gail and her husband, the legendary Clay Felker.

I've been blessed to have so many important mentors in my life. Lanny Davis took me under his wing when I was all of 21 years old. From The George Washington University, Steven Livingston and Frank Sesno have been there for me in more ways than I can count.

Whenever I teach a class or guest lecture, I try as best I can to mimic Steven Livingston, but nothing can beat the original.

A special thanks to everyone at Warburg Realty, including its president, Frederick Peters. Leslie Hutchings read over early drafts of the book and provided tremendous feedback.

My family was very important in the creation of this book. I would turn a chapter in to my wife, telling her it was complete. And then three days later I would throw the chapter out and start all over again. She read each "final" version, and provided great insights. My parents, Dennis and Shelley Haber, were equally important as part of my feedback loop team.

Lastly, I want to thank all the sources who participated in this book. You are a very special collection of social entrepreneurs, academics, doers, dreamers, and true believers.

—Jason Haber
New York City
November 22, 2015

# about the author

Jason Haber is a serial and social entrepreneur. His extensive career has intersected the worlds of business, politics, academia, and technology. In 2010 he co-founded Rubicon Property, a social entrepreneurial real estate firm based in Manhattan. Warburg Realty acquired the firm in 2014. He has vast experience in government and public policy. He has worked as an advisor for several elected officials and candidates in New York City and in Washington, DC. Haber served as an adjunct professor at John Jay College where he taught a public policy course. He is a board member of Rivet Media, a virtual reality startup. Haber is a frequent commentator on CNBC and Fox Business News and has been covered in *The New York Times* and *The Wall Street Journal*. He holds a bachelor's degree in Political Communication from The George Washington University and a master's degree from the School of International and Public Affairs at Columbia University. Haber currently lives in New York City with his wife and daughter.

# index